# Compassion In Action

A LEADERSHIP PARADIGM
THAT CULTIVATES ORGANIZATIONAL
HAPPINESS

Lars Kure Juul

Clearsight Publishing
Copenhagen

Clearsight Publishing
Copenhagen
GntlGiant.com

Ordering Information:
Quantity sales. Special discounts are available on quantity purchases by corporations, associations, and others. For details, contact the publisher.

Compassion In Action / Lars Kure Juul. —1st ed.
ISBN 978-87-971055-4-2

# Contents

*To The Gentle Giants!*

*This book is dedicated to leaders who aspire to be the gentle giants of their organizations and societies, creating a future where humanity and compassion lead the way.*

"The next big revolution isn't driven by technology - it's driven by more humanity and COMPASSION IN LEADERSHIP.

Our real problems aren't technological; they are moral and ethical."

# The Brief

This first chapter serves as *The Brief* — an "executive summary" of the book. If you want to grasp the core concepts quickly, this section will give you the foundation you need.

Think of *The Brief* as your leadership compass, offering clarity on Compassion in Action, The Happiness Sweet Spot, and the leadership principles that cultivate Organizational Happiness.

This book expands and builds on my previous book, *Organizational Happiness*[1], I introduced the idea that happiness, when approached strategically through The Happiness Sweet Spot as an enabling platform, becomes a driving force for organizational success.

We explored the pillars of purpose, strengths-based leadership, and compassion, showing how these elements

---

1 *Organizational Happiness: The Happiness Sweet Spot & Your Motivational Landscape, Amazon worldwide.*

intersect to create the Happiness Sweet Spot - an environment where people and organizations perform at their best.

This new book builds on that foundation. While *Organizational Happiness* focused on the broader framework for creating engaged and high-performing workplaces, *Compassion in Action* zooms in on one of its most potent and transformative pillars: Compassion.

This book is not just about the *why* behind leadership and well-being - it is about the *how*. *Compassion in Action* is the applied methodology that brings *Organizational Happiness* to life, making it tangible, measurable, and actionable.

While *Organizational Happiness* defines the vision of a thriving workplace, *Compassion in Action* provides the strategic framework and leadership behaviors that translate this vision into everyday practice. It is the bridge from strategy to action - ensuring that purpose, strengths, and compassion are not just ideals but embedded in the culture, leadership, and decision-making processes of an organization.

COMPASSION IN ACTION

"An interest in understanding other peoples difficulties and a burning desire to do something about it!"

By integrating *Compassion in Action*, leaders cultivate environments where people feel valued, engaged, and empowered - unlocking both human potential and sustainable success.

This book is deeply personal to me—it's Heart Work. I see an urgent need to support leaders and organizations in recalibrating their leadership compass, ensuring that caring for the well-being of the people they serve and lead becomes a strategic priority.

Our real problems are not technological but moral and ethical. People generally know what to do, but some get distracted by ego, money, or fear.

The challenge for leaders is no longer to find a good reason that compassion is good for business. The challenge now is to design work and workplaces that awaken compassion and facilitate compassionate leadership in the best way.

Compassion In Action is a win-win-win. For the individual, for the organizations and for our societies.

And as the Dalai Lama says about compassion, "It is the ultimate source of success in life."

We spend over 90,000 hours of our lives at work. As leaders, we must – and I think it's an obligation and a responsibility - create environments that promote well-being and happiness. It is also good business and high performance. This is Compassion in Action.

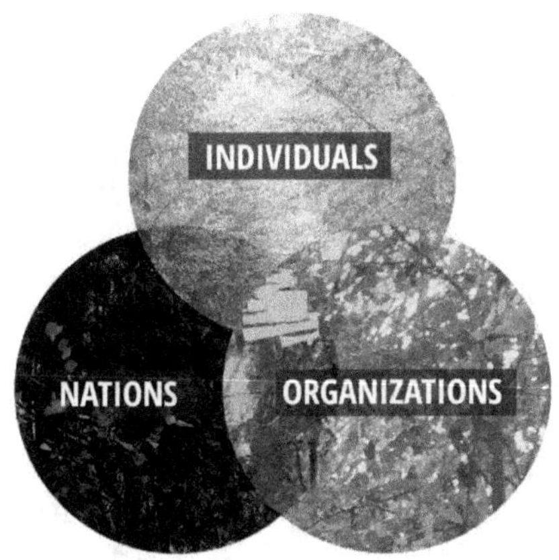


*Compassion In Action serves all. Source: Lars Kure Juul*

All aspects of life are interconnected, with blurred and complex borders between work, life, business, customers, and society.

The world is changing faster, more unpredictably, and more profoundly than we've seen in generations. Technological advancements have redefined how we work, live, and connect, while social, environmental, and economic challenges have brought an urgency for organizations to evolve beyond profit-driven metrics. Amid this whirlwind of change and transformation, one timeless concept has emerged as both a guiding principle and a powerful competitive advantage: compassion.

For those leaders who master compassion, I use the term *Gentle Giant* as a metaphor or symbolic term. They serve as role models and beacons of Compassion in Action as a leadership paradigm.

"We take care of the well-being of the
people we serve and lead.

It's an obligation.

And we understand that it's a huge
opportunity for sustainable success for
the organization we are responsible for.

We are GENTLE GIANTS."

Compassion should not be seen as a soft, optional value to hang on the walls of a company headquarters. It's about making the case for the well-being of the people we lead and serve a real strategic priority, and doing so in a strategic, intentional way. It's a huge opportunity to take care of the well-being of the people we lead and serve allowing them to create extraordinary results and outstanding business.

Compassion also means being in service. To the people you lead and to the future. A concept closely tied to Servant Leadership, which will be explored further in this book. Leaders today must embrace their role as stewards of tomorrow, shaping strategies and cultures that prioritize long-term success, well-being and sustainability over ego driven gains and siloed, short-term gains.

This includes a renewed focus on the well-being of the people we lead and serve, while acknowledging that it presents a significant opportunity for the organizations we are responsible for. It provides a strong business case and a motor for sustainable success.

If you do it right, it will be your unique competitive advantage.

I'll explore how compassion as a mindset, a skill, and a strategy can transform organizations and empower leaders to navigate complexity while fostering thriving, sustainable workplaces.

"Your real, **UNIQUE COMPETITIVE ADVANTAGE** is in your Purpose, your Culture and how you Manage and Lead your people"

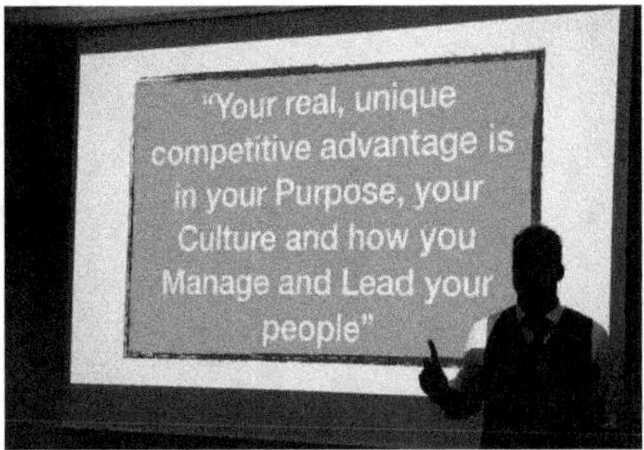


*From a Keynote in South Africa*

This book is my invitation to tap into the power of compassion: for the individuals, for organizations, and for society.

Compassion, as I see it, is the catalyst that brings purpose to life, amplifies the impact of strengths, and creates a culture where people feel seen, valued, and empowered. As I defined in *Organizational Happiness*: Compassion is about having an interest in understanding the difficulties of others and a burning desire to help them overcome those challenges. It is this blend of empathy and action that makes compassion so impactful in organizational and leadership contexts. It is a motor for sustainable success.

It's not just about being kind; it's about being deliberate in fostering connections, addressing challenges with empathy, and making choices that reflect both care and courage.

This book is meant as a conversation starter. I offer some enabling frameworks for leaders to get from strategy to action, but I don't claim to have all the answers. Instead, I focus on asking the right questions to inspire meaningful conversations and reflections.

"Follow those who ASK THE RIGHT QUESTIONS, not those who claim to have all the answers."

This book will also focus on the critical transition from strategy to action, answering the strategic question: How do we effectively cultivate a culture of compassion in our organization?

The book is designed to be as practical as it is inspirational. Throughout, you will find:

- Research-Based Insights: Drawing from neuroscience, psychology, and organizational studies, we'll uncover why compassion works and how it can be operationalized in modern organizations.

- Real-World Examples: I will examine how leaders and teams have implemented compassion-based strategies to drive innovation, improve well-being, and achieve exceptional results.

- Actionable Frameworks: You will gain tools, models, and guidance for embedding compassion into your leadership style, organizational culture, and business strategy.

- Personal Reflection: Each chapter will include opportunities for introspection, encouraging you to explore your own relationship with compassion and how you can use it to inspire those around you.

Why focus on compassion now?

Because the challenges we face today demand more than technical solutions. They require human solutions. Research and the work I'm doing with leaders and organizations consistently shows that organizations with compassionate cultures outperform their peers. But beyond the data, compassion creates something more profound: a sense of belonging and purpose.

Consider this: in a world increasingly driven by automation and artificial intelligence, what will set organizations apart is not how efficiently they can process data, because that will be handled much more effectively by computers. It is how effectively they can build trust, foster collaboration, and unlock and release the full potential of the people who will use the data and who are needed to add meaning, sense, reason and empathy. Compassion In Action is the key to unlocking these outcomes.

Over the years, I have had the privilege of working with thousands of leaders and international organizations, guiding them to explore and implement Organizational Happiness and Compassion In Action.

Through these experiences, I've witnessed firsthand how a focus on humanity and compassion can unlock remarkable potential and drive sustainable success.

Central to this is the recognition that taking care of the well-being of the people we lead and serve is not just a moral obligation but a strategic advantage.

As I discussed in my previous book, *Organizational Happiness*, purpose, strengths-based leadership, and compassion are pillars that create thriving workplaces. This next step is about delving deeper into compassion's transformative power as a leadership paradigm.

I hope this book inspires you to calibrate your leadership compass - a metaphor for aligning your actions and decisions with a deep sense of purpose and care for those you lead and serve. I assure you - this will not only drive exceptional results but also bring a profound sense of fulfillment to your professional life.

While this book primarily centers on organizational and business leadership, I strongly believe that global leaders - presidents, prime ministers, and policymakers—must also recalibrate their leadership compass to navigate today's complex challenges with wisdom and compassion.

Although this isn't the primary topic of this book, I hope it creates a ripple effect, inspiring global leaders to adopt a more compassionate, humanity-driven approach to addressing societal challenges.

> "Many of the challenges we face are not technology-driven or market-driven; they are morally and ethically driven. The solution is rooted in humanity and compassion."

This book is an invitation to join a movement and a tribe of *Gentle Giants*—leaders who prioritize compassion as a core element of their leadership and cultivate exceptional organizational cultures. These Gentle Giants are committed to building workplaces where humanity, care, and purpose drive success and create lasting impact and sustainable success.

In service to the future, leaders must recognize that their actions today echo far beyond immediate outcomes. It is both their duty and a chance to shape organizations that prioritize the well-being of individuals while driving sustainable success.

The book is a call to action for leaders, teams, and organizations to embrace compassion not as a buzzword, but as a transformative practice. We'll start by defining compassion for the organizational context, moving beyond surface-level niceties to uncover its deeper, strategic value. From there, we'll dive into the practical; how-to cultivate compassionate leadership, design systems that prioritize well-being, and create cultures where compassion is woven into the fabric of daily operations. Is in our organizational DNA.

After reading the book, my hope is that you will not only see Compassion In Action as a powerful tool for organizational success but as a guiding principle that can help you lead with greater authenticity, impact, and humanity.

On a soft note, with reference to this crazy world we live in right now, this leadership paradigm also sparks hope.

Many of the leaders I work with share a common sentiment: Compassion in Action is not only transformational, - it brings hope. Hope for workplaces that cultivate trust, belonging, and engagement. Hope for leaders who inspire, empower, and serve. Hope for a future where real leadership is defined by compassion, courage, authenticity, and human connection.

"This book is dedicated to leaders who aspire to be the gentle giants of their organizations and societies, creating a future where humanity and compassion lead the way."

"Getting from Strategy → Action!

The Answer Is: SIMPLE!

Complexity is the enemy of execution"

I take pride in being a practitioner - focusing on what actually works in real life.

Leadership, happiness, and compassion are not just theories or abstract ideals; they must be translated into action to create real impact.

Often, my role is to bridge the gap between intention and implementation - helping organizations move from talk to action, from strategy to execution, from commitment to behavior change.

I see myself as a changemaker, guiding leaders and teams to embed Compassion in Action into the fabric of their organizations.

Happiness and compassion can be complex topics, and organizations themselves are complex organisms. One of the important messages I emphasize in leadership development and training, particularly through the Global Organizational Happiness Certification Course with UPEACE, is: "Complexity is the enemy of execution."

If we overcomplicate leadership and culture-building, real change never happens. That's why Compassion in Action must be clear, practical, and measurable - something leaders can embed into daily decision-making, team interactions, and organizational strategy.

This is also why compassion should not be reduced to an "employee service" or a feel-good initiative. It must be a strategic priority—a leadership force that drives engagement, performance, and sustainable success.

Making it a strategic priority means being clear on three key aspects:

1. What we should do as leaders – Defining the leadership behaviors that cultivate trust, engagement, and a thriving culture.
2. How we do it – Embedding compassion into our leadership practices, decision-making, and organizational culture.
3. How to integrate and ignite – Moving from intention to action by ensuring compassion is woven into our leadership approach, performance metrics, and daily interactions.

When compassion is treated as a core leadership responsibility, not just a supportive initiative, it becomes a catalyst for unlocking human and organizational potential—driving both well-being and business success.

Compassion isn't a luxury; it's the key to building thriving organizations where people feel valued, empowered, and ready to contribute their best.

# Foreword

"Daring leaders work to make sure people can be
themselves and feel a sense of belonging."
— Brené Brown

I met Lars for the first time in Costa Rica more than a decade
ago. He had traveled from his home in Copenhagen to the
University for Peace in Costa Rica to attend a workshop
titled "Positive Leadership." From our first conversation, it
was clear that Lars was not just another participant—he was
someone deeply committed to the principles of leadership
that prioritize people, purpose, and positive impact. His
diverse background as a lawyer, CEO, international HR professional, C-level consultant, and author gave him a unique
perspective on the challenges and opportunities facing
today's leaders. But what struck me most was his belief that
leadership should not only drive performance but also cultivate human flourishing – and that could only happen with
deep compassion.

Over the years, our professional paths have crossed more
times than I can count, and we have been co-developing and
co-facilitating workshops for leaders. His passion for bringing
more humanity into leadership has been evident in every

conversation, project, and initiative he has undertaken. It is this passion that has led to *Compassion in Action: A Leadership Paradigm That Cultivates Organizational Happiness* - a book that is both timely and necessary.

In an era of rapid change, uncertainty, and increasing workplace disengagement, leaders can no longer rely solely on traditional models of authority and control. Instead, they must embrace a new paradigm—one that recognizes compassion not as a soft skill, but as a strategic priority for sustainable success.

This book is a powerful call to action for leaders to recalibrate their approach, making the well-being of their people not just a corporate initiative, but a foundational leadership principle.

Lars masterfully integrates cutting-edge research, real-world leadership experience, and proven frameworks to show that compassion is not just an ethical imperative- it is a competitive advantage.

He introduces the *Compassion in Action Model*, a practical three-step leadership approach that guides leaders in embedding compassion into their strategies, culture, and decision-making processes. Through compelling case studies, insights from influential thought leaders, and evidence from top research institutions, this book makes a strong business case for compassionate leadership.

But beyond the strategies and research, what makes this book truly impactful is its invitation to a movement. Lars challenges us to step up as leaders who embrace courage, authenticity, and service. He reminds us that the next big revolution in leadership is not technology-driven - it is about bringing more humanity into the workplace.

Reading *Compassion in Action* is not just an intellectual exercise; it is a call to lead differently. Whether you are an executive, entrepreneur, or aspiring leader, this book will challenge you to reflect, reframe, and take action.

I am honored to introduce this work and to call Lars a friend and collaborator. His vision for leadership aligns deeply with the mission of the University for Peace and its Centre for Executive Education - to develop leaders who drive meaningful, sustainable change in the world.

I invite you to read this book with an open mind and a willingness to act. Because when leaders embrace compassion, they don't just transform their organizations—they create environments where people and purpose thrive together.

Mohit Mukherjee
Founding Director
UPEACE Centre for Executive Education

# Introduction

Before we dive into Compassion in Action as a force for sustainable success, it's essential to establish a shared understanding of the key concepts that lay the foundation for this leadership approach.

The following section is a revised excerpt from my #1 international bestseller, *Organizational Happiness*. If you're already familiar with the Happiness Sweet Spot and the Motivational Landscape, or if you have been trained in the framework and are actively using it within your organization, feel free to skip ahead. However, if you are new to these concepts, I strongly encourage you to take a moment to explore them here.

Understanding Organizational Happiness, the Happiness Sweet Spot, and the Motivational Landscape will provide you with the right foundation for integrating Compassion in Action into your leadership and workplace culture. These concepts are not just theoretical. They are practical, research-based frameworks that drive engagement, performance, and sustainable success.

By grounding ourselves in Organizational Happiness, we can more fully appreciate how Compassion in Action serves as a transformative leadership force. One that fosters belonging, well-being, and long-term organizational excellence and sustainable success.

# CHAPTER 1

# The Happiness Sweet Spot

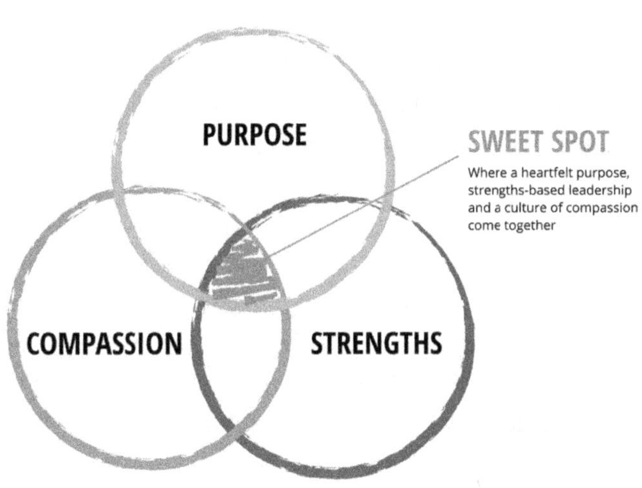

We need to talk about organizational happiness. We need happy organizations, happy people, and happy nations. A happy organization is a high-performing organization. Because a happy person is healthy and productive, the business case for organizational happiness is a "no-brainer."

So, even if you don't think ensuring happiness is part of your job as a leader, make it your responsibility because it's good business. Organizational happiness will be your competitive advantage - no doubt about it.

But I believe we need to look at people and organizations from a different perspective and recognize that for most people, "the pursuit of happiness" is very real and relevant—it's their life and it's our life.

I think part of an organization's role and responsibility is to facilitate and create an environment and leadership culture that makes happy employees. I don't think happiness is a private, individual thing. It's certainly a responsibility for our society and nations,[2] but organizations should take responsibility for the happiness of people, too—and not just as part of a corporate social responsibility strategy.

Organizational happiness can be difficult for some leaders and professionals to address. I find in my experience as an advisor and HR professional that we often find it easier

---

2 The United Nations' Sustainable Development Goals are easily linked to happiness for individuals, organizations, and society.

to talk about "employee engagement," "motivation," or "staff satisfaction" than about "organizational happiness"—which from my perspective is what employee engagement, motivation, and staff satisfaction are all about.

The Happiness Sweet Spot and your Motivational Landscape—the frameworks and enabling tools in this book—give you a way to work with organizational happiness and employee engagement so that you have a competitive advantage. It is my hope that this will show you a compelling and easy path.

So why is it that you have not done this already?

As leaders, we experience an overflow of information. We get confused, and there are academic supporting arguments for any direction you might want to take or any decision you make. Right or left. Right or wrong.

I have seen this materialize in what I would call "paralyzed leadership." There is always doubt, a second opinion, and a reason to wait. We sit on our hands.

Making decisions is not easy. As a leader you have already delegated most of the decision-making, or your organization has already made the easy decisions.

That means you are left with the tough decisions—the ones that, if you seek advice or ask around, will always generate a "second opinion." This makes you lose power and speed.

At the same time, the world and the dynamics in our markets are moving so fast that if you don't move, you are toast.

Recent research[3] has shown that when you ask CEOs if they have doubts about making the right strategic decisions or doubt their own abilities to make the right people decisions, the number who say yes is rising dramatically with the speed of change and information (over)flow. When asked, "Do you ever doubt yourself?" in a 2015 survey, 71 percent of the respondents said yes.

The paths to the future are made, not found.

To be successful, we need to turn strategy into action. Now. Fast.

I believe that as leaders, we need to be able to reduce complexity and use simple tools with simple rules[4] and heartfelt values and beliefs—so that we dare to lead.

The research, the academic work, and the case studies are already there. I want to give you a framework to work with organizational happiness: *the Happiness Sweet Spot*. And I will give you a way to measure, monitor, and follow up on organizational happiness and employee engagement. That is your *Motivational Landscape*.

---

3 The CEO Report: Embracing the Paradoxes of Leadership and the Power of Doubt (Heidrick and Struggles) is a good place to start if you want to dive into this subject.
4 An inspiring book on this topic is *Simple Rules: How to Thrive in a Complex World* (2015) by Donald N. Sull and Kathleen M. Eisenhardt.

The Happiness Sweet Spot and your Motivational Landscape make up an enabling platform and a framework within which to work with organizational happiness, to operationalize your strategy, and to get you from strategy to action and behavior. It's simple, powerful, and fast. Some leaders call it "a strategy for people decision-making."

The Happiness Sweet Spot is a powerful and unique idea, because it presents what we already know in a simple model that works and is easily actionable. That's it!

It's difficult to talk about organizational happiness without grounding it in some of the academic work and research that makes it legitimate to refer to happiness in organizations as a premise for high performance and success.

In the past two decades, the study of emotion, emotional intelligence, and related topics has grown significantly.

One of the emotions that psychologists have studied most intensively is happiness. Organizational psychologists, economists, and neuroscientists have joined in learning more about it. These disciplines have distinct but intersecting interests: Psychologists want to understand what people feel, economists want to know what people value, and neuroscientists want to know how people's brains respond to rewards and so on. Having three separate disciplines all interested in a single topic has put that topic on the scientific map.

Papers on happiness are published in the journal *Science*, people who study happiness win Nobel Prizes, and governments all over the world are rushing to figure out how to measure and increase the happiness of their citizens.

Even nations focus on happiness. Gross National Happiness (also known by the initialism GNH) is a philosophy that guides the government of Bhutan. It includes an index that is used to measure the collective happiness and well-being of a population. Gross National Happiness was instituted as the goal of Bhutan's government in the constitution of Bhutan enacted on 18 July 2008.

Also, in 2011, the UN General Assembly passed Resolution "Happiness: toward a holistic approach to development" urging member nations to follow the example of Bhutan and measure happiness and well-being and calling happiness a "fundamental human goal."

From an organizational point of view, we are talking about "The Happiness Dividend,"[5] the Happiness Sweet Spot, and the business case for organizational happiness.

A lot of the research confirms things we already know or at least does not surprise us: People who are in good romantic relationships are happier than those who aren't. Healthy people are happier than sick people. People who participate in their community are happier than those who don't. Rich people are happier than poor people. And so on.

Why is this interesting for organizations? Because happy people are more creative and more productive.

---

5 Shawn Achor, "The Happiness Dividend."

In the introduction I promised that this book would be a guide from strategy to action, so I will not spend a lot of time on the academics. I will just conclude that the science of happiness is a real thing. And it makes sense for individuals, organizations, and nations to pursue happiness, because it leads to wealth, health, innovation, and productivity.

All that means that there is a great case to be made for organizational happiness in business. But also, we simply need more happy people and happy societies on our earth, in my opinion. It will make a better world.

For that, a good, simple model is the PERMA model, developed by Martin Seligman.

Psychologist Dr. Martin Seligman, widely viewed as the father of positive psychology, asserts that happiness (he also uses the terms *well-being* and *flourishing*) is about five elements, which can be captured by the acronym PERMA:

- **Positive** emotions—feeling good
- **Engagement**—being completely absorbed in activities
- **Relationships**—being authentically connected to others
- **Meaning**—purposeful existence
- **Achievement**—a sense of accomplishment and success

He describes and elaborates on the model in his 2011 book *Flourish*.

## A New Theory of Well Being

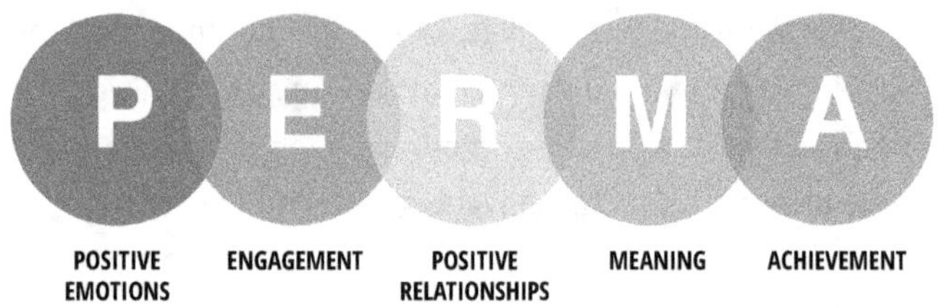


Martin Seligman's research and case studies are also relevant in an organizational context.

People are still people when they go to work. And we saw from research that happy employees perform better and produce better results. So, it is quite interesting to dive into what makes people happy and put it in an organizational context. That is what we do in the Happiness Sweet Spot model.

The five elements of the PERMA model can help people reach a life of fulfillment, happiness, and meaning. It can almost be characterized as a "life hack" if you try and apply it to you own life and reflect on each of the 5 elements; "Is there an area of my life I need to give more attention?

I use that model as a scientific reference for building your organizational happiness strategy and establishing your Motivational Landscape.

The PERMA model can be applied to organizations when we know the correlation between happiness and employee engagement and performance.

The organizational perspective is what we offer with the Happiness Sweet Spot framework and the three pillars of organizational happiness.

I describe the model in detail in chapter 3 of *Organizational Happiness*, but in short, it establishes that happiness in organizations happens when a heartfelt purpose, strengths-based leadership, and a culture of compassion come together in a sweet spot where the full potential of the organization is unleashed.

In the following chapters, I will dig deeper into and explore the reasons for making organizational happiness a strategic priority.

"COMPASSION IN ACTION and Organizational Happiness aren't just "wellbeing programs".

It has to be a clear strategic priority.

It's about tapping into the power of The Happiness Sweet Spot and truly taking care of the well-being of the people we lead and serve.

It's both an obligation and a huge opportunity and motor for sustainable success for the organizations we're responsible for."

My own journey with taking happiness seriously really started in 2010 with an academic interest in the science of happiness in connection with implementing strategies for employee engagement. I started reading everything I could find on the topic.

In June 2011 the author Shawn Achor wrote an article for the *Harvard Business Review* titled "The Happiness Dividend," and in 2012 *HBR* dedicated an issue to happiness called The Value of Happiness.[6]

That really got me inspired, and I dived into the science of happiness with the purpose of understanding it and helping organizations apply it in an operational way.

In 2014 Mohit Mukherjee[7] and I started an initiative called "Just Do Happy" to help facilitate ambitious organizations creating real strategies for organizational happiness. I also posted a LinkedIn article that year on "5 Reasons Why Happiness and Well-Being Will Be Relevant for You in 2015." It got a lot of attention in only a few days.

That told me that leaders and organizational professionals were curious about the subject. But still, in 2014 organizational happiness was perceived and implemented as

6 Harvard Business Review, January/February 2012.
7 Mukherjee is founding director of the UPEACE Centre for Executive Education in Costa Rica.

celebrating successes, doing a lot of high-fives, and having a soccer table in the office.

In 2015 we launched the Happiness Sweet Spot to inspire leaders and organizations and offer a framework and a structure for working seriously with organizational happiness. This has allowed us to meet many amazing, inspiring people, and I have had the privilege of helping organizations work on making happiness a strategic part of creating a high-performing organization with a competitive advantage.

This work has generated multiple insights into developing tools and models for implementing strategies for organizational happiness.

When we work with organizational happiness and employee engagement, the first question is "How do we do it?" That is the theme of the book *Organizational Happiness*, and the book takes a deep dive into what really works related to compassion as a leadership paradigm.

The second question when we implement strategies is "How do we know if our strategy is working as intended?" Your yearly employee engagement survey will not tell you that as it's a snapshot of old data and not an up-to-date key performance indicator (KPI) of organizational happiness and employee engagement.

And a feeling is not enough. You can't rely on gut feelings only and out-of-date data when you make decisions about people and are monitoring one of your most important strategies for success.

Therefore, we developed a simple tool: Your Motivational Landscape[8] measures happiness and engagement as a KPI for our partners on a regular basis with a pulse survey using ten simple and relevant questions.

Below is an "executive summary" of my Happiness Sweet Spot model, including the 10 key questions used in the Motivational Landscape to measure, monitor, and follow up on Organizational Happiness.

I'm sharing this here because it serves as the foundation and enabling framework for Compassion In Action.

Together, the Happiness Sweet Spot and Motivational Landscape form a powerful combination for translating strategy into action. Turning intentions into tangible behavior change.

---

8 www.MotivationalLandscape.com

This framework isn't just conceptual; it's backed by a structured infrastructure designed to track progress and drive meaningful organizational transformation.

Below, I will briefly touch on each of the three pillars of Organizational Happiness and explore a bit more about WHAT compassion is and how it looks in a leadership and organizational context.

If you're looking for a deeper understanding of The Happiness Sweet Spot and the Motivational Landscape, I encourage you to explore my book, *Organizational Happiness*, or reach out to me. I have a wealth of practical cases, data, and research that I'd be happy to share. There is so much happening in this space—leaders stepping up as role models, lighthouses, and inspirational thought leaders.

Additionally, I invite you to explore the Global Organizational Happiness Certification Program at UPEACE[9], the UN-mandated University for Peace. This program provides in-depth training on these concepts and equips leaders with the tools to embed organizational happiness and compassion into their leadership approach.

If you're interested in learning more or applying these frameworks in your organization, reach out - I'm happy to help.

---

9 University for Peace (UPEACE). (n.d.). Global Organizational Happiness Certification Programme. Retrieved from UPEACE Centre for Executive Education

To work strategically with happiness in your organization, you need to break it down and develop strategies and facilitate actions in three main areas:

1.  Purpose
2.  Strengths
3.  Compassion

We use the term *the three pillars of organizational happiness.* I will explain and elaborate on each of these as we go forward.

So, what is the Happiness Sweet Spot? You're in the Organizational Happiness Sweet Spot when you've found the place where your strategies and efforts around purpose, strengths-based leadership, and cultivating a culture of compassion come together, support one another, and are integrated.

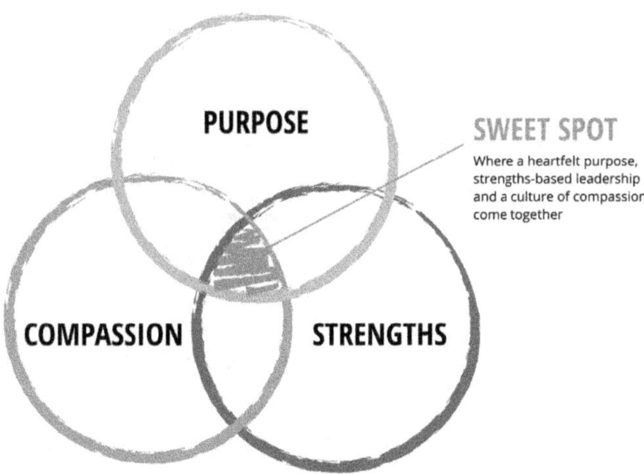

When you ignite the sweet spot and, as leader, unlock the full human potential of the organization, your organization will be "fully charged".

And it relates directly to the PERMA model I referenced earlier:

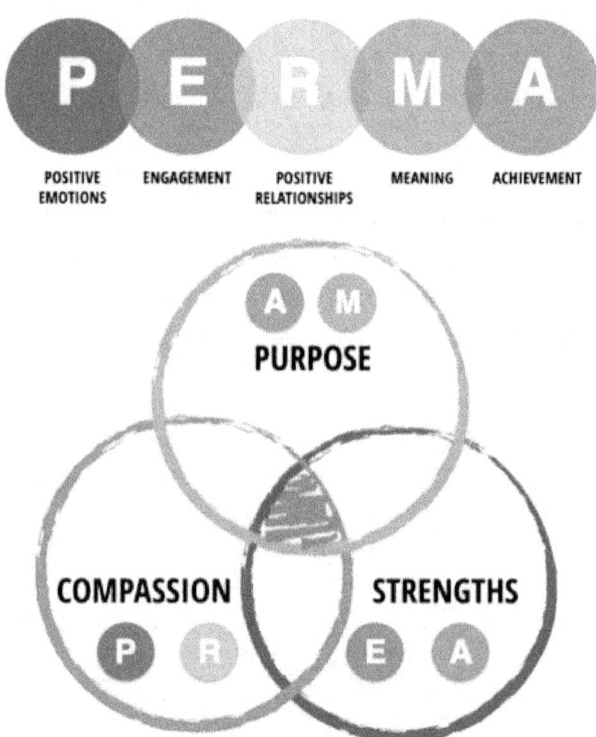

# Purpose

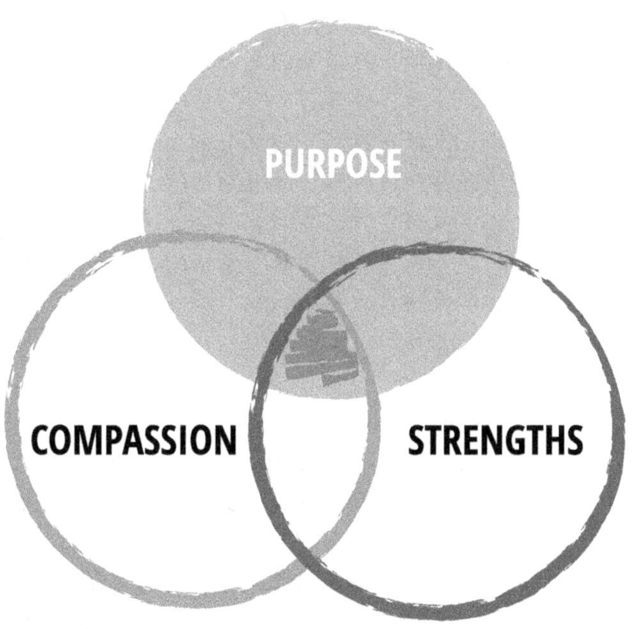



*The first pillar of organizational
happiness is purpose.*

Purpose is your organizational *why*.

It's a heartfelt "reason for being" that is bigger than profit. When market conditions are right, companies can be successful with a pure profit purpose. But a lot of potential is released when it's more than that.

When your purpose is clear, many other things get easier: your storytelling to customers about why to buy, attracting the best people to your organization, and more.

On the individual level your *why* brings meaning, which is the *M* in the PERMA model I introduced earlier.

When it is really good, your organizational *why* resonates—does not conflict—with the personal *why* of the people in the organization.

- Purpose brings meaning.
- Having a purpose is a competitive advantage.
- Your purpose becomes your brand as an employer.

You need a strong purpose to attract and retain top talent. If you don't have that, your organization will struggle and not last.

For some organizations a heartfelt purpose and *why* comes easily and naturally. For other organizations it is a bit of a stretch to come up with a "meaningful" purpose.

Scandinavian Tobacco Group's promise is "We create moments of great enjoyment for smokers."[10]

The PepsiCo mission statement is as follows: "Our mission is to be the world's premier consumer products company focused on convenient foods and beverages. We seek to produce financial rewards to investors as we provide opportunities for growth and enrichment to our employees, our business partners and the communities in which we operate. And in everything we do, we strive for honesty, fairness and integrity."[11]

The mission statement of Patagonia is as follows: "Build the best product, cause no unnecessary harm, use business to inspire and implement solutions to the environmental crisis."[12]

Which one would you like to give your best to? What company would get the best part of you? Which company would you talk about with pride at a cocktail party?

For Scandinavian Tobacco Group and PepsiCo, my best guess is that they have to attract top talent with a promise of exceptional professional development, above industry salary, and retain talent with contractual bindings. This can be a successful strategy, but it's really hard work—not heart work.

---

10 www.st-group.com/en/our-company.
11 http://www.pepsico.com. The mission statement is from 2013.
12 https://www.patagonia.com/company-info.html.

Of course, that would depend on the actions and actual behavior those companies put behind their statements.

But the stronger and more heartfelt the purpose, the easier it is for employees to give all they have, to want to work there, to relate to and be proud of it. It makes us happy on a personal level.

# Strengths

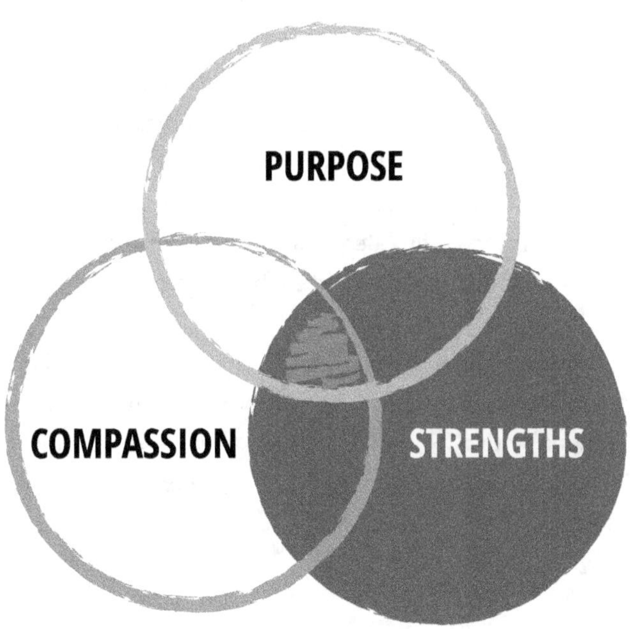



*The second pillar of organizational
happiness is strengths.*

The second pillar of organizational happiness is strengths-based leadership and real talent management. That means discovering people's talents, strengths, and potential and putting them into play for your organization.

Focusing on strengths and what's working well will result in the highest employee engagement.

- Conversations about strengths reveal the super-powers in an organization.
- Effective talent management recognizes that everybody has talent, potential, and strengths.
- Strengths-based leadership unlocks an organization's potential.
- A successful talent management strategy requires simple processes and enabling tools.

It's no surprise to you as a leader that ignorance results in the lowest engagement. A focus on problems and what's not working, with a fix-it attitude, leads to higher engagement. But it's not nearly as high as the engagement that is stimulated by a strengths-based leader.

# Compassion

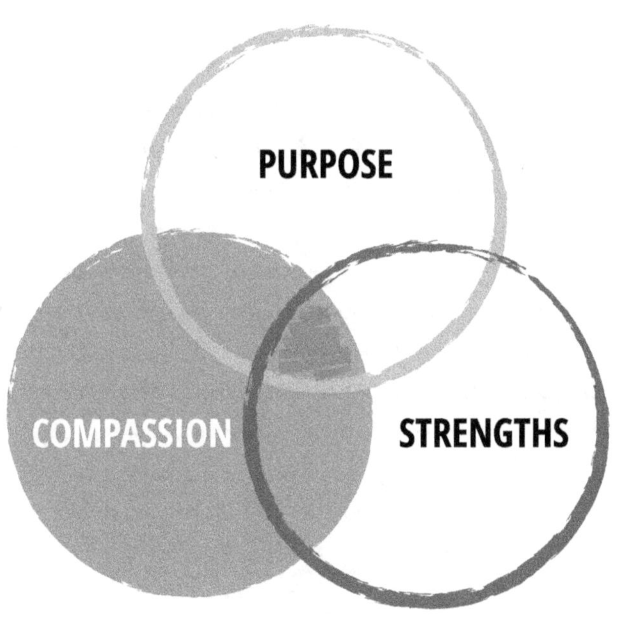


*The third pillar of organizational
happiness is compassion.*

Compassion means people are interested in understanding the difficulties of other people and have a burning desire to help them.

- Compassion and curiosity increase employee loyalty and trust.
- Compassion boosts team performance by helping employees feel "safe."
- Compassion facilitates the spirit of experimentation and is critical for creativity.

The way I see it, compassion is about leadership and leadership is about compassion. If you aspire to be an effective leader, you can't do it successfully without compassion.

Research has demonstrated that even before establishing their own credibility or competence, leaders who project warmth are more effective than those who lead with toughness. Compassion, kindness, and warmth accelerate trust, which is a building block for performance and teamwork.

This will be explored further in the following chapters.

---

When you work with the three pillars of organizational happiness as an engine for sustainable success, you need to know if you've hit the sweet spot for your organization. Do you put the right emphasis on each of the pillars? What works best for your unique situation in your organization? Are your efforts paying off?

# Your Motivational Landscape

If you work strategically with organizational happiness and Compassion In Action as an engine for sustainable success, you need to know if you are within the sweet spot.

You need to know, "How are we doing right now? ".

Because you wouldn't and can't rely on gut feelings alone.

Your Motivational Landscape[13] is a simple pulse survey and tool that tells you about the state of your organizational happiness and employee engagement—in real time.

---

13 www.motivationallandscape.com

The tool is connected to the three pillars in the Happiness Sweet Spot, so you can measure, monitor, and follow up on your activities and purpose, strengths, and compassion.

Your Motivational Landscape is built on research and case studies on what creates and is conducive to organizational happiness, employee engagement, and high performance. Behind the scenes we have built in the PERMA model and the science of happiness, because they are fundamental to this.

It consists of ten unique questions related to organizational happiness and employee engagement, asked on a regular basis. The results are reported on a dashboard and provide important data your business depends on for its success.

## The 10 Questions in Your Motivational Landscape

Based on my work with the Happiness Sweet Spot, the science of happiness, and research on employment engagement, we have developed and carefully designed ten questions or statements that we know are related to organizational happiness and employee engagement. We are of course inspired by what other organizations and researchers have been developing in this area.[14]

Each of the questions is designed to be conducive to the three pillars of the Happiness Sweet Spot, organizational happiness, and employee engagement.

We can relate each of the questions to a research-based *why*, and each question is related to purpose, strengths, and compassion.

1.  I feel happy at work.

**PURPOSE**

2.  I'm proud of being part of my organization.
3.  I know how I contribute to the mission of our organization.
4.  I would recommend a friend for a job here.

**STRENGTHS**

5.  I have the opportunity to do what I do best.
6.  I have opportunities to learn, grow, and develop.

---

14 Gallup's Q12 and some of the great work done by Nic Marks and his team at Happiness Work are good resources for inspiration in this area.

7. I have the resources available that enable me to do a good job.

## COMPASSION

8. I feel people care about me.
9. I get recognition or praise (I am appreciated).
10. My opinion counts.

Every question is accompanied by an optional link where employees can elaborate by responding to these two prompts:

- What worked well?
- It would be even better if...

A constant focus on your Motivational Landscape will engage employees in the pursuit of organizational happiness. Happiness needs to be on the agenda and in conversations at the lunch table and the cocktail party.

Motivational Landscape gives us the data that allow us to manage and lead our people. Because we can and will lead. We dare to lead.

We want to see smoke before it becomes a fire. And we want to share best practices and learn from the best in the organization.

We developed Motivational Landscape because we identified a need to make better people decisions instead of relying on gut feelings when it came to developing strategies for organizational happiness and employee engagement.

Based on interviews with leaders and professionals and our work with the Happiness Sweet Spot implementation, we came up with a simple platform that tells us how we are doing and allows us to measure, monitor, and follow up—as if our people matter as much as our financial performance and our customer satisfaction.

The storytelling on the Motivational Landscape purpose can be captured in the following.

Although most organizations have systems and tools to measure, evaluate, and track financial performance and customer satisfaction, many still lack a clear, up-to-date picture of organizational happiness and employee engagement.

However, over the last five years, there has been significant progress in how organizations value and leverage real-time data. More leaders now recognize the importance of frequent pulse surveys, monthly engagement tracking, and real-time insights to understand and improve workplace well-being. At the same time, the tools and systems available on the market have improved considerably, making it easier than ever to gather meaningful, actionable data on employee experience, motivation, and overall organizational health.

This shift reflects a growing awareness that engagement and well-being are not static metrics but dynamic factors that require continuous attention—just like financial performance and customer satisfaction. Organizations that actively track and respond to this data are better positioned to culti-vate a thriving, high-performing workplace.

The annual employee engagement survey or staff satis-faction survey does not do that for you. Those processes and reports produce a snapshot of the situation in your organi-zation. And by the time you have that snapshot, it's typically three months old.

Would we accept old data on financial performance?

No, we wouldn't—and we don't.

We have systems and tools in place to report almost in real time how we are doing on financial performance. So why do we accept old data delivered once a year on organizational happiness and employee engagement, when we know it is—or should be—one of our top three strategies for success?

It beats me. When I talk to my organizations about this dilemma, what I hear is excuses for not investing in measuring organizational happiness and employee engagement, and a need for guidance so that "we don't create another heavy HR-process monster that demands a lot of attention and resources from the organization."

If you are afraid of that – make it short, make it simple, make it automated, make it integrated in the other processes you have, make it real time.

Because it is difficult to focus your efforts and develop a strategy for organizational happiness if you don't know how you are doing.

A few good questions to ask yourself:

Do you have clear picture of the employee engagement, motivation, and happiness in your organization?

Do you have a clear, up-to-date picture of the Motivational Landscape across your organization?

If not, how do you find out? And how do you set up a simple feedback system that gives you the data you need in an effective way, without burdening your employees?

I think you should ask your employees at least once a month.

Use your own survey system, look at the pulse surveys in the market, or take advantage of the work we have done for our clients in this area.[15]

The market for pulse surveys is relatively new.[16] In the beginning I saw many offerings that were driven by "tech nerds" and not so much by "people and leadership nerds." In my view this has led to solutions for employee engagement surveys that are over-engineered. The market is starting to mature in the sense that service providers in this area are

---

15 See www.MotivationalLandscape.com.
16 Bersin, "A New Market Is Born."

starting to provide simple, no-nonsense solutions to having data on employee engagement. Because that is what most organizations need to drive engagement and make the right people decisions.

If you explore the market for pulse surveys, my advice would be to look out for unnecessary complexity and difficult-to-understand algorithms and make sure that questions and surveys are based on science and backed by professionals.

We want to see smoke before it becomes a fire.

And we want to share best practices and learn from the best in the organization.

---

Before we dive into *Compassion in Action* as a leadership paradigm, it's important to first explore what compassion truly means and how it takes shape within organizations.

Understanding this foundation will provide the necessary context for applying compassion as a strategic and measurable force in leadership and your organizational culture.

# Compassion

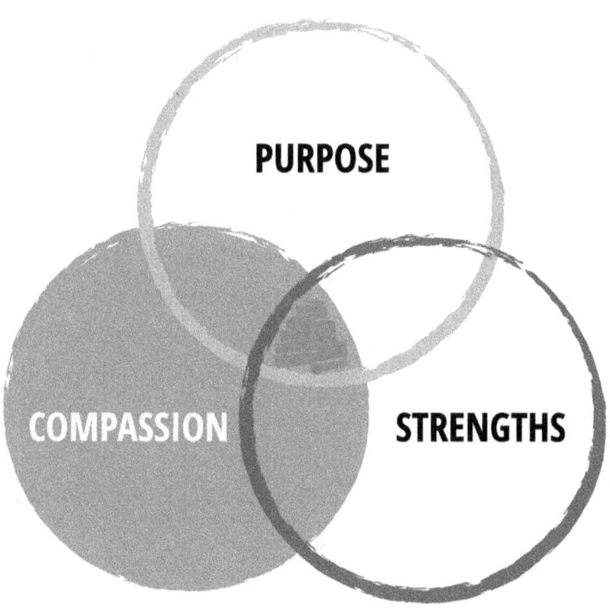


*The third pillar of organizational happiness*

What does it mean to cultivate a culture of compassion? Culture is about "the way we do things around here" and how we treat each other. And in a culture of compassion people in the organization are genuinely interested in understanding the difficulties of other people and having a burning desire to help them.

The way the organization is integrating and cultivating compassion is defined by your leadership and culture. That's it!

I believe that the key to a happier and more successful society is the cultivation and growth of compassion at every level—individual, organizational, and national. And it starts with taking the lead and striving for it.

In this chapter I look at compassion as part of culture and as a leadership discipline or style. I explore what compassion is, what it looks like in organizations, and why cultivating a culture of compassion is good for business, contributing to its performance and success.

We often hear that culture is your competitive advantage.

But what is culture really about? At its core, culture is shaped by your people, the behaviors of your leaders, the individuals you welcome into the organization, the actions and attitudes you refuse to tolerate, the daily habits that define your workplace, and the shared sense of purpose that drives everything forward.

Compassion is a fundamental human emotion that impacts how your company culture will be perceived. It has often been overlooked in organizational development and leadership practices.

Many organizations attempt to shape behavior through standard operating procedures and policies. But true leadership goes beyond rules—it requires fostering a culture where compassion is an integral part of how people lead, collaborate, and drive success. Because we also need to tap into the fundamental human emotions when we want people to thrive and be the best possible version of themselves.

Your company culture is either compassionate or it isn't. If it isn't, you're likely missing the opportunity to discover and cultivate your Organizational Happiness Sweet Spot.

But if you are able to cultivate a culture of compassion, you have taken a grand step toward your Organizational Happiness Sweet Spot.

Although compassion may not always be the first word that comes to mind when discussing leadership, competitive advantage, business models, or building a high-performing organization, it should be. You and your shareholders need that edge—the kind of advantage that comes from unlocking the full potential of people who are engaged, empowered, and committed to a shared purpose.

And I think this is becoming a trend. Organizations and societies look for something "more," something more "right" and more genuine, where we serve and take care of each other and our employees. That is compassion.

As mentioned earlier, research[17] has demonstrated that leaders who project warmth are more effective than those who exude toughness, even before credibility and competence are taken into account. Kindness and warmth evoke trust, which is a building block of performance and teamwork.

This is important. As leaders we should know what good leadership looks like and what bad leadership looks like in our organization. We should recognize good leadership behavior and know what behavior is not acceptable.

Researchers at Oxford University analyzed hundreds of published papers that studied the relationship between kindness and happiness. They uncovered twenty-one studies that explicitly prove that being kind to others makes us happier. Added to that is research from the University of Warwick that revealed that happy people are 12 percent more productive at work than unhappy people. I will elaborate further on the business case in chapter 3.

*"Love and compassion at work? Really?"*

That's a question I hear often, as the evidence of business case for happiness at work is still not common sense or a "no-brainer" for organizations.

---

17 See the work of Amy Cuddy and her research partners at Harvard Business School.

Sometimes it's followed by something like, "This happiness crap is one thing...and now you want us to have love and compassion at work too? I'm not sure our board would think it's a good idea or something we should invest in."

I think that attitude or train of thought is a sign of mediocre leadership and a mistake. It's playing it safe. When we look at our organization and our employees as "resources" that need to be managed—i.e., human resource management—we are being mediocre and getting mediocre results.

Leadership is also about courage. Dare to lead, put yourself and your heart into it, and set an example for how we treat each other: with love and compassion—even at work.

So be that exceptional leader and create exceptional results.

I will give you the arguments for why cultivating a culture of compassion is a good idea for you and your organization or business.

Some companies and organizations already know firsthand that love and compassion have a place at work and have a strong influence on workplace outcomes.[18] The more love our employees feel at work, the more engaged they are and the happier they are.

In organizations and at work, what we want is "companionate love," which is far less intense than romantic love.

---

18 Barsade and O'Neill, "Employees Who Feel Love Perform Better."

Compassion is based on warmth, affection, and connection rather than on passion.

As we define it in the Happiness Sweet Spot, compassion is "an interest in understanding the difficulties of other people *and* a burning desire to help them."

I think that captures leadership at its best.

Some leaders are afraid of being too personal and too closely connected with others at work, because they think their behavior can or will be misunderstood.

I understand that concern. But cultivating a culture of compassion is possible only if you feel warmth, affection, and connection—at work.

And you need to combine that culture and leadership style with a solid moral compass and strong personal values. Your strengths are your superpowers. Your values act as the compass you use to decide what to do with those superpowers.

There is a connection to and an overlap with what we call "servant leadership."[19] Servant leadership is a leadership philosophy in which the main goal of the leader is to serve. A servant leader shares power, puts the needs of the employees first, and helps people develop and perform as highly as possible.[20] I will explore the leader as servant in chapter 4 where

---

19 The term servant leadership was coined by Robert K. Greenleaf in "The Servant as Leader," an essay first published in 1970.
20 Autry, The Servant Leader.

I'll be sharing three enabling frameworks for Compassion In Action.

A culture of compassion is evident "when colleagues who are together day in and day out, ask and care about each other's work and even non-work issues," Sigal Barsade says. "They are careful of each other's feelings. They show compassion when things don't go well. And they also show affection and caring—and that can be about bringing somebody a cup of coffee when you go get your own or just listening when a co-worker needs to talk."

When I am a keynote speaker and conducting workshops on "how to cultivate a culture of compassion,"[21] my experience is that in some cultures and countries, compassion is easily understood, and its value is instantly accepted. It's the most natural thing—part of people's upbringing and teaching.

In some countries and cultures, however, compassion is not accepted or understood. I find this mostly in northern Europe and parts of the United States.

So, my message is this: Dive into compassion if it sparks something in you. Or just see compassion as leadership in its essence - an authentic, genuine, and real kind of leadership.

Compassion is leadership and leadership is compassion!

---

21 I have experience speaking about compassion in Pakistan, South Africa, the Nordic countries, Europe, Latin America, Saudi Arabia, Asia, and the United States.

## Terrorism and Peace Building in Asia

I have seen compassion being a differentiator many times in my career. Over a period of ten years, I was engaged as an expert and advisor in a troubled region in Asia related to leadership, capacity building, counterterrorism missions, and peace building.

I worked closely with police and prosecutors on counter-terrorism initiatives to enhance cooperation so that terrorists could be prosecuted more effectively.

It is of course an intense environment—very macho and conflict/fight oriented. You need to have a strong *why* and personal purpose to flourish in that setting.

In the beginning of the missions we all focused on professional competencies like human resource management, key performance indicators, leadership, project management, and so on. We only really scratched the surface when we delivered the reports and documented capacity building and results.

I found it difficult to facilitate the cooperation and teamwork. We were tackling conflict and peace building without a sense of trust and connection—without compassion.

This changed over the years as I worked on these projects. We were able to build trust so that conflicts became opportunities to grow and connect.

That didn't happen by itself.

One of the simple things I did was set up informal meetings and dinners with small groups of people (five to eight) with the theme "My Dream." Just that. At those "dream meetings" we shared personal stories about our lives, families, and dreams for a better future. We followed three guidelines: (1) Be present as you listen to other people's dreams, (2) don't try to "fix" other people's dreams, and (3) know you can offer to help.

I deliberately went first at these "dream meetings" and put all my heart into these conversations. I emphasized love and compassionate leadership: understanding the difficulties of others and having a burning desire to help them.

My observation and experience were that this completely changed the environment and "culture" around the important stuff we wanted to succeed with. There was less fighting, and people were more inclined to set aside their personal agendas. And there was more compassion and cooperation.

We were a lot more effective and successful with our mission when there was love and compassion among us.

We unlocked the potential.

I was given the nickname "the Gentle Giant from Denmark," something for which I was very grateful. Later, when they asked me to come and help on missions, some of the guys said, "We need the Gentle Giant here to help us out."

When we treat ourselves and others compassionately, we tend to come together in a contributory manner that raises the group to greater heights as a whole. With this, bonds are formed, trust is established, and a willingness to work together on projects and have a shared vision becomes the driving force behind our intentions.

## Why Compassion?

Cultivating a culture of compassion is relevant and important for the wellbeing of the people we lead and serve and for the sustainable success of the organization we are responsible for.

In the next chapter, I will explore why Compassion in Action is more than just a concept—it is a leadership style defined by specific habits and behaviors. I will also discuss why embracing this approach is essential for creating a thriving, high-performing organization.

Compassion increases employee loyalty, and trust boosts individual and team performance by being conducive to feeling "safe." Compassion facilitates the spirit of experimentation and is critical for creativity and innovation.

According to research,[22] employees who felt they worked in a loving, caring culture reported higher levels of satisfaction and teamwork. They showed up to work more often.

---

22 Barsade and O'Neill, "Employees Who Feel Love Perform Better."

Approximately one in five adults in the United States—43.8 million, or 18.5 percent—experience mental illness and/or depression in a given year. This is a scarily high rate. The main cause of depression is not a lack of material necessities but being deprived of the affection of others.[23] What if this number could change dramatically by changing our workplaces?

However, compassion cannot stand in isolation. Policies and processes also help define "the way we do things around here." When it comes to building and nurturing a strong organizational culture, it's important to strike a balance. Being overly rigid with processes and formalized procedures can stifle flexibility and innovation. My advice: keep it structured but adaptable—apply a light touch to ensure culture evolves naturally while still providing clear direction.

But that is not leadership. That's called managing resources. It does not release and unlock potential.

If you as a leader want high performance—plus organizational happiness and high employee engagement—you will have to take the sometimes-difficult role of creating an environment where there is room for the crazy, unique superpowers so that you can use them for your mission and strategy. And sometimes you have to build a team around those superpowers, because those superpowers are needed to do something new or extraordinary. And sometimes those superpowers need to be cultivated and supported – without being destroyed or overlooked in the process.

---

23 National Institute of Mental Health. "Prevalence of Any Mental Illness."

Many successful companies are focusing on compassion.

Whole Foods Market has a set of management principles that begin with "Love." PepsiCo lists "caring" as its first guiding principle on its website. Zappos also explicitly focuses on caring as part of its values: "We are more than a team though—we are a family. We watch out for each other, care for each other, and go above and beyond for each other."

When people come together in a supportive environment and feel safe from competition, there is less fear. There is less fear of failure, which results in better creativity, innovation, and performance. The feeling of being psychologically safe enhances performance.[24]

When we cultivate a culture of compassion, we facilitate an environment and a leadership culture where "I trust that it's OK to make mistakes."

The more we care for the well-being and happiness of others, the greater our own sense of well-being becomes.

Fostering a culture of compassion—where people genuinely care for and support one another—creates a sense of ease, reducing fears and insecurities while strengthening resilience. This not only benefits the organization, employees, and overall performance but also enhances your own well-being as a leader.

---

24 Duhigg, "What Google Learned From Its Quest to Build the Perfect Team."

As the Dalai Lama says about compassion, "It is the ultimate source of success in life."

We can strive gradually to become more compassionate—that is, we can develop both genuine interest in and sympathy toward our employees' difficulties and the will to help them. As a result, we as leaders feel better and stronger.

## Cultivate a Culture of Compassion

Cultivating a culture of compassion is simple, yet human emotions and organizational behavior and development always come with complexity. No two organizations and no two leaders are the same.

Your organization is a unique organism, and your employees are unique human beings with their own motivations.

One size does not fit all. And leadership means choosing to dive into the complexity and diversity without having all the answers. But you can bravely cultivate a culture that is conducive to sustainable success.

As a leader, you have the ability to cultivate a culture of compassion. If you don't, your organization risks missing out on a powerful competitive advantage that drives engagement, performance, and long-term success. It takes courage and heart to lead. It means practicing your values, choosing courage over comfort, and daring to lead.[25]

Compassion is shown in the small moments between employees - a warm smile, a kind note, a sympathetic ear—day after day, month after month, helping to create and maintain a strong culture of compassion and leading to employee engagement, productivity, and customer satisfaction.

Support, practice, and facilitate that as a leader.

On the other hand, organizational messages that endorse winning at all costs or prioritizing self-promotion undermine compassion in your organization.

As compassionate leaders we should be telling stories about our organization's purpose and *why*. We should inspire employees by talking about our organization's accomplishments, emphasizing its desire to make the world better and our commitment to doing good.

The capacity to deeply relate to others is key to all forms of relational success—at work and at home. If you are a leader, notice this: Leaders who give the least amount of positive guidance to their subordinates are less successful in achieving their organizations' goals, and their employees are unhappier with their work. By not taking an active role in dialogue and team building, you generate more interpersonal conflicts within groups.

---

25 Brené Brown has done inspiring research and framed leadership in her book *Dare to Lead: Brave Work. Tough Conversations. Whole Hearts.*

Most of the decisions we make on any given day are not derived from a rational mind-set but from a response to our emotionally driven network of mirror neurons, where we seek commonality with those around us and connection to the work we do.

And that means that compassionate leadership includes a genuine, honest, and humble approach that allows us to tap into the superpowers, strengths, creativity, and insights of our employees. It could be as simple as saying, "I don't know" or "I need help."

To effectively lead others, we need to show our employees that we are present to hear, understand, and provide what they require to succeed and thrive under our compassionate leadership. And we cannot fake it.

---

I work with leaders and organizations to help them find and cultivate their Organizational Happiness Sweet Spot, linking it directly to their leadership practice and environment.

Over the past five years, my experience—and the experiences of the leaders I've worked with—has revealed a key insight:

*Compassion is easy to understand but difficult to consistently put into practice without leadership training and guidance.*

While most leaders recognize the value of compassionate leadership, many struggle to integrate Compassion in Action into their daily leadership practice and organizational culture. Research suggests that compassion isn't something you're necessarily born with. Instead, it can be developed through practice.

That's why, coming from the foundation of The Happiness Sweet Spot and the Motivational Landscape, it's essential to explore Compassion In Action, how it manifests in leadership, and how we can intentionally integrate it.

In the following chapters, I will provide practical guidance, tools, and frameworks to help leaders integrate Compassion in Action into their leadership approach and tap into its transformative power. I will also reference the work of leading thinkers and researchers in this field, whose insights have helped shape this essential leadership paradigm.

One critical aspect of compassion that also deserves deeper exploration is self-compassion - a foundational practice for any leader striving to lead. And also enhances trust, engagement, and well-being across entire organizations. I will explore this in chapter 6.

Understanding the Happiness Sweet Spot gives us a foundation for thriving organizations, but true transformation happens when leaders move beyond strategy and take intentional action to unlock the full human potential of the organization. This is where Compassion in Action becomes essential - not as a theoretical concept, but as a leadership approach and paradigm that actively fosters trust, engagement, and sustainable success.

Let's dive in.

# Compassion in Action

Compassion is a Leadership paradigm that cultivates Organizational Happiness. "We take care of the well-being of the people we serve and lead. It's an obligation. And we understand that it's a huge opportunity for sustainable success for the organization we are responsible for."

Leadership is not just about authority, making decisions, or achieving results.

A *leadership paradigm* is more than a leadership style - it is a fundamental way of thinking and practicing leadership. It shapes how leaders make decisions, interact with their teams, and drive organizational culture.

Compassion in Action is not just about the "soft" leadership; it is a powerful, strategic approach that shifts leadership from a position of power to a commitment to service - where well-being, trust, and psychological safety become essential drivers of high performance and sustainable success.

## COMPASSION IN ACTION

"An interest in understanding other peoples difficulties and a burning desire to do something about it!"

To *cultivate* in the context of Compassion In Action means to nurture, grow, and develop with intention and care.

Cultivating organizational happiness through Compassion in Action is about embedding compassion into leadership practices, fostering trust, engagement, and a deep sense of belonging. It is an active process - one that requires conscious effort, continuous learning, and the courage to lead with both heart and accountability.

In this chapter, we will explore what it truly means to integrate Compassion in Action into leadership, how it transforms organizations, and why great leadership is not about knowing all the answers - but about creating the conditions where people and organizations can thrive.

Great leadership is not about transformation.

Great leadership is about unlocking and releasing potential.

Transformation, Disruption and Change are words full of action, energy and movement. And - if not managed exceptionally well - it creates uncertainty, unpredictability, doubt, reservation and anxiety in our organization. That's why performance, engagement and employee well-being suffer in many transformations.

Unlocking and releasing the potential we already have in the organization by tapping into the power of Compassion In Action is a gentle paradigm and approach that builds on trust, psychological safety, strength-based leadership, and a deep commitment to the well-being of the people we lead and serve.

This is the real motor for transformation and sustainable success.

What sets leaders who successfully build and cultivate a compassionate environment apart?

They focus on sustainable success, ensuring the well-being of the people within their circle of influence.

Their leadership is not about power but about creating lasting impact, leaving behind a legacy that future generations can be proud of.

True leaders understand that compassion in action is the key to real, sustainable success.

I call these leaders Gentle Giants—those who lead with purpose, courage, wisdom, and compassion. We will get back to those.

"It's already there!

COMPASSION IN ACTION is a powerful key to unlock and release the potential in your organization.

Great leadership is not about transformation.

Great leadership is about unlocking and releasing potential.

This is the real motor for transformation. And a motor for sustainable success."

## Why Compassion in Action

As previously stated, Compassion increases employee loyalty, and trust boosts individual and team performance by being conducive to feeling "safe." Compassion facilitates the spirit of experimentation and is critical for creativity and innovation. It makes people want to do their best.

Leadership isn't about being soft. You can demonstrate warmth while taking responsibility and showing care—care for the well-being of the people you lead and serve, care for your customers, and care for delivering meaningful results.

Sometimes, the most compassionate choice is to remove a toxic individual from the team or to transition someone into a role better suited to their strengths and personality. However, these decisions should always be made with empathy, integrity, and a genuine commitment to what is best for both the individual and the organization. Let your heart guide the way.

Lets look into the Business Case and the competitive advantage and strategic impact. In my opinion prioritizing the well-being of the people we serve and lead is not just an ethical responsibility - it's a strategic necessity. This is not just about employee satisfaction or a feel-good philosophy; the data consistently shows that organizations with a strong commitment to well-being, psychological safety, and compassion outperform their peers in key business metrics.

A recent McKinsey Health Institute report highlights that investing in employee well-being can unlock nearly $12 trillion in global economic value.

The business case for this investment is clear:

- Higher productivity – Healthy, engaged employees perform significantly better.
- Lower absenteeism – Reduced sick days and burnout-related drop-offs.
- Reduced healthcare costs – Lower medical claims from stress-related illnesses.
- Increased engagement and retention – Employees stay longer where they feel valued.
- Stronger ESG (Environmental, Social, Governance) positioning – Investors and stakeholders prioritize companies that prioritize well-being.

This aligns directly with my core message:

*"We take care of the well-being of the people we serve and lead. It's an obligation. And we understand that it's a huge opportunity for sustainable success for the organization we are responsible for."*

Compassion in Action is a building block for trust, which in turn is a building block for psychological safety. Psychological safety is the single most critical factor for high performance in teams, as highlighted in Google's Project Aristotle study. The research found that the highest-performing teams were those where members felt safe to take risks, be vulnerable, and share ideas without fear of embarrassment or retribution.

Organizations that embed psychological safety into their leadership approach benefit from:

- Increased innovation – Employees feel empowered to share creative ideas.
- Stronger collaboration – Teams communicate openly and work together more effectively.
- Higher resilience – Employees navigate challenges and setbacks more effectively.
- Better decision-making – Inclusive discussions lead to more well-rounded strategies.

When we cultivate a culture of compassion, we create an environment where employees trust that it's okay to make mistakes, learn, and grow. This facilitates a leadership culture that fosters innovation, accountability, and continuous improvement.

In *Organizational Happiness*, I detailed concrete data on the impact of prioritizing happiness and engagement in the workplace. Research from Gallup, Martin Seligman, and other thought leaders provides compelling evidence:

- 8–18% increase in performance and productivity
- 2–10% higher customer satisfaction and loyalty
- 6–73% lower employee turnover
- 7–37% reduction in absenteeism
- Up to 300% more innovation
- 14–29% increased profit
- 10–19% higher sales
- Up to 400% reduction in stress and burnout

- 23–59% fewer safety incidents
- 6–27% improvement in quality and fewer defects/errors

These numbers paint a clear picture: Organizational Happiness and Compassion In Action is not just the right thing to do - it's a high-performance strategy. Organizations that prioritize happiness, well-being, and psychological safety create thriving workplaces, resilient teams, and sustainable business success.

The future of leadership isn't just about efficiency and output - it's about cultivating workplaces where people can thrive. By embracing Compassion in Action, leaders unlock the full potential of their teams, build trust, and create the psychological safety necessary for long-term success.

This is not just an idea—it's a leadership imperative. The data is clear: Compassionate organizations outperform their competitors. The leaders who understand this will be the ones who drive sustainable success and make a lasting impact.

## What Really Works

Here are nineteen things you can do to cultivate an organizational culture of compassion and develop your compassionate leadership skills.

Sometimes I call these micro habits for leaders that aspire to cultivate a culture of compassion.

*Pay attention.* Look for clues that might suggest someone is suffering—body language, tone of voice, or unusual work patterns—and ask gently in a private setting what might be going on.

*Practice presence.*[26] In my opinion, this is by far the most important of all leadership skills. If you are able to be here, now, and listen and serve, you can move people and organizations. We are easily distracted and are surrounded with tools and electronics that make being present hard. And even though presence and compassion are what people need, there becomes less of it. Be that present leader. Don't hide in emails, diagrams, and KPIs. Say good morning, go for lunch, and practice listening and serving.

*Be available.* Create opportunities for connection. Keep your door open, stay a little while after meetings, put away your phone, walk and talk, be curious and empathic.

*Take compassionate action.* Make employees feel safe. Send them a short note. Ask, "How's life?" and be present and show that you want to hear the answer. Offer work flexibility that suits people's family situations. Again, be present, empathic, and available.

*Think about the emotions you're expressing to employees every day.* Your mood creates a cultural blueprint for the group.

---

26 If you are interested in this, a good publication is Aware: The Science and Practice of Presence—A Complete Guide to the Groundbreaking Wheel of Awareness Meditation Practice, by Daniel J. Siegel.

*Look at your policies and management practices.* Are they conducive to compassion? Do you talk about compassion?

*Encourage cooperation, not competition,* even through subtle cues.

*See people as individuals,* not as a number or resource. Look at how you do and present reporting. Acknowledge employees' strengths and positive attributes in front of others.

*Don't play the blame game.* When we blame others for their misfortune, we feel less tenderness and concern toward them.

*Notice and savor how good it feels to be compassionate.* As a leader you feel better and stronger when you practice compassion.

*Don't be a sponge.* When we completely take on other people's suffering as our own, we risk feeling personally distressed, threatened, and overwhelmed; in some cases, this can even lead to burnout. Instead, try to be receptive to other people's feelings without adopting those feelings as your own.

*Create a team-working environment.* Encourage brainstorms and mastermind meetings. Invite the team to share in the organization's vision and goals and help create action steps to achieve them. An environment where you can collaborate by sharing ideas and offering creative solutions is one that thrives.

*See your employees beyond the roles they play in your organization.* Don't treat your employees as a "human resource" or "human capital" or cogs in the organizational wheel, but as full participants in your shared purpose.

*Inspire daily acts of kindness.* Hold a brainstorming session or challenge teams to come up with daily acts of kindness. When these acts come from the heart and are authentic, they will help spark and fuel a culture of compassion.

*Organize team-building activities.* This is an opportunity to feel included and connect. Take the lead or ask for a volunteer to set up team-building activities for employees.

*Admit that you don't know everything.* It's impossible for anyone to truly know or understand the complexities of what our organization has to address or overcome. If we walk around thinking we are the only ones with enough experience and knowledge to know what needs to be done, how can we truly listen to and understand what our employees face, not to mention what it's really like to work for us?

*Align Roles with Strengths.* Match people with roles that leverage their unique talents and superpowers, ensuring they feel engaged, capable, and fulfilled in their work.

*Recognize and Guide Growth,* Provide clear, constructive feedback that highlights what employees are doing well while offering guidance on how they can further develop and excel.

"*COMPASSION IN ACTION* and Organizational Happiness aren't just "wellbeing programs".

It has to be a clear strategic priority.

It's about tapping into the power of The Happiness Sweet Spot and truly taking care of the well-being of the people we lead and serve.

It's both an obligation and a huge opportunity and motor for sustainable success for the organizations we're responsible for."

*Share Knowledge and Experience.* Foster a culture of learning by openly sharing your insights, expertise, and resources, empowering others to grow and succeed

Great leaders understand that *Compassion in Action* starts from within. To be truly effective in your leadership role, you must first cultivate compassion toward yourself. I often meet leaders who constantly push themselves, saying, "*I should be doing more,*" or "*I could have done better.*" This mindset of "*not enough*" can be draining, limiting both energy and impact.

The above micro habits for leaders is a good start to help cultivating a culture, by small changes in habits and behavior.

For some, these habits come naturally—for others, not as much. But as I mentioned earlier, they can be learned. In chapter 4, I share three proven frameworks that effectively drive Compassion in Action as a catalyst for Organizational Happiness and sustainable success.

When you practice self-compassion, you shift from self-criticism to self-awareness. You recognize your efforts, maintain a strong and clear presence, and communicate with authenticity—creating the kind of leadership that truly inspires action.

In Chapter 7, I will explore self-compassion as a foundation for Compassion in Action and how it fuels sustainable, impactful leadership.

# CHAPTER 4

# 3 Enabling Frameworks

Cultivating Organizational Happiness and tapping into the power of Compassion in Action requires more than good intentions. Leaders also need practical guidance and the ability to build micro-habits that embed compassion into daily leadership practices.

In my experience, this is necessary—but not sufficient.

To make Compassion in Action a true leadership paradigm and a strategic priority, we need effective enabling frameworks that translate intention into action.

In this chapter, I present three proven frameworks that work in practice:

The Compassion in Action (CIA) Model
The Power of Belonging
The Leader as Servant

"Getting from Strategy ⟶ Action!

The Answer Is: SIMPLE!

Complexity is the enemy of execution"

These frameworks have been successfully implemented with thousands of leaders and organizations, providing a simple yet effective approach to embedding Compassion in Action into leadership and culture.

## The CIA Model
### A Three-Step Leadership Model for Compassion in Action

This three-step model provides a structured approach for leaders to embed compassion into leadership in a way that is actionable, measurable, and transformational.

At the core of this framework is a three-step process that helps leaders operationalize Compassion in Action:

1. Identify WHO You Are – The journey starts with self-awareness and authentic leadership.

2. Define the CONTEXT You Are In – Understanding the organizational culture, external landscape, and people dynamics.

3. Assess the READINESS of Your Organization – Ensuring alignment and fostering action-oriented change.

### Step 1: Identify WHO You Are

*"Leadership begins with self-awareness."*

Great leadership starts from within. Leaders must first understand themselves before they can effectively lead others. This means reflecting on:

- What are my core values?
- What motivates me as a leader?
- How do I respond to stress and challenges?
- Am I leading with authenticity?

Understanding oneself as a leader can be supported by psychometric tests and strengths assessments that provide valuable insights into leadership tendencies, communication styles, and areas for growth. Some widely used tools include:

- Clifton Strengths (Gallup) – Helps leaders identify and leverage their natural talents.
- MBTI (Myers-Briggs Type Indicator) – Provides insights into personality types and leadership preferences.
- DISC Assessment – Focuses on behavioral styles and effective communication.
- The Big Five Personality Traits – Measures key characteristics that influence leadership effectiveness.
- Emotional Intelligence (EQ-i 2.0) – Assesses emotional intelligence, a critical factor in compassionate leadership.

Why Self-Awareness Matters

- Authenticity: Teams trust leaders who are genuine and transparent.

- Emotional Intelligence: Awareness of one's own emotions fosters empathy and better decision-making.
- Resilience: Self-aware leaders manage stress and setbacks more effectively.

Practical Applications for Leaders

1. Reflection and Journaling – Regularly evaluate leadership habits and impact.
2. Seek Feedback – Engage in 360-degree feedback from employees and mentors.
3. Clarify Your Purpose – Define what truly matters to you as a leader.

A leader who knows WHO they are can lead with confidence, integrity, and Compassion in Action. They leverage their strengths while also managing their weaker areas, finding balance by being self-aware and intentional. Rather than letting limitations hold them back, they complement their abilities by collaborating with others whose strengths fill the gaps, creating a well-rounded and high-performing team.

## Step 2: Define the CONTEXT You Are In

*"Great leadership is about understanding the environment you operate in."*

Leadership does not exist in a vacuum. To effectively practice Compassion in Action, leaders must understand the people, culture, and external influences that shape their leadership landscape.

Key Contextual Factors to Consider

- Organizational Culture: What are the shared values, behaviors, and leadership norms?
- Industry Trends: How do external economic, technological, and social factors impact employee well-being?
- Psychological Safety: Does your workplace encourage open communication, trust, and inclusivity?

Practical Strategies for Leaders

1. Cultural Assessments – Use surveys or team discussions to gauge workplace culture.
2. Stakeholder Engagement – Listen to employees, customers, and key stakeholders to understand expectations.
3. Adaptive Leadership – Recognize that different teams and situations require different leadership approaches.

Use the Motivational Landscape Assessment – This tool provides insights into what truly drives and engages people within an organization. By mapping out individual and collective motivators, leaders can align strategies with what energizes their teams, ensuring a more meaningful and sustainable leadership approach.

Compassionate leadership is context-dependent. Leaders who understand the cultural and organizational landscape can tailor their leadership style to meet the needs of their teams.

## Step 3: Assess the READINESS of Your Organization

*"Compassion in Action is only effective when teams are ready to embrace it."*

A compassionate leader can only be as effective as the systems, people, and culture that support them. This step ensures that the team and organization are aligned and ready for change.

Key Readiness Indicators

- Openness to Change: Do employees feel psychologically safe to embrace a new leadership approach?
- Structural Support: Do HR policies, leadership frameworks, and decision-making structures support well-being and compassion?
- Sustainable Action Plans: Are there clear steps to integrate compassion into leadership behaviors and company policies?

Practical Strategies for Leaders

1. Conduct Readiness Surveys – Assess how employees feel about leadership, psychological safety, and well-being.

2. Pilot Compassionate Leadership Practices – Test small-scale initiatives.

3. Measure Impact – Track key metrics such as employee engagement, trust levels, and turnover rates.

4. Use a Motivational Landscape Assessment – for insights into what truly drives and engages people within an organization. By mapping out individual and collective motivators, leaders can align strategies with what energizes their teams, ensuring a more meaningful and sustainable leadership approach.

When Compassion in Action is supported by organizational readiness, it moves beyond philosophy and becomes a practical, measurable, and sustainable leadership strategy.

*"What you do will make a difference; you just need to go and decide what difference you want to make."* —*Dr. Jane Goodall*

## The Power of Belonging

If you do this right, this is where retention, high performance, and real employee engagement lives.

Belonging is a fundamental human need, deeply intertwined with our sense of identity, purpose, and connection. As Abraham Maslow famously noted, belonging is foundational to human motivation, sitting just above physiological and safety needs in his hierarchy. In the workplace, a sense of belonging is more than a "nice-to-have"; it is a driver of engagement, innovation, and resilience. Yet, in today's fast-paced and fragmented world, fostering belonging has become both more challenging and more critical than ever.

Compassion lies at the heart of belonging. Compassionate leadership sees and values individuals not only for their roles but for their humanity. It creates a culture where employees feel trusted, respected, and supported. This chapter explores the transformative power of belonging, supported by academic research, practical insights, and my personal experience working with thousands of leaders and organizations worldwide, including Boston Scientific.

At its core, this is an invitation to embed belonging as a fucus area and strategic priority—unlocking human potential and driving sustainable organizational success.

Belonging has been described as "the feeling of being seen, valued, and included" (Coqual, 2020). Research

## THE POWER OF BELONGING

"To be *Seen*, to *Contribute* & to be *Proud*."

consistently demonstrates its profound impact on organizational outcomes.

A few data points on this:

- Higher Performance: Employees with a strong sense of belonging show a 56% increase in job performance and are 75% less likely to take sick days.
- Enhanced Engagement: Workers who feel they belong are three times more likely to stay with their employer and recommend their workplace to others.
- Retention and reduced Turnover: Organizations with high belonging save millions annually in turnover costs, with some case studies estimating savings of over $52 million for a 10,000-person company.

Despite these benefits, a striking 40% of employees report feeling isolated or excluded at work, leading to decreased engagement and well-being. These figures underscore the urgency for leaders to address belonging as a core organizational priority.

Through my work with leaders and organizations, I have developed a practical framework for fostering belonging and getting from strategy to action.

My model serves as an effective enabling platform to transition from strategy to action on the "Power of Belonging". By operationalizing these principles, leaders can directly integrate compassion into their day-to-day practices, embodying

Compassion in Action in ways that yield measurable outcomes and transformative cultural shifts.

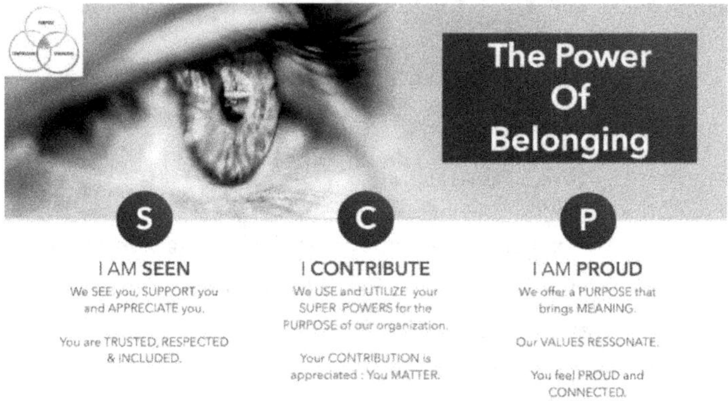


This model is built on three key pillars:

1. Seen: Employees feel recognized, respected, and valued for their unique contributions. They experience trust and inclusion.
2. Contribute: Employees understand how their strengths and skills are utilized to advance the organization's purpose. They know their contributions matter and what is expected from them
3. Proud: Employees feel proud to be part of an organization whose values resonate with their own. They experience a sense of connection and meaning in their work.

This framework has been successfully applied across various industries, including our collaboration with more than 1,000 leaders at Boston Scientific, a global company with 48.000 employees worldwide.[27]

By integrating these principles, organizations have created cultures where individuals thrive, and teams achieve exceptional results.

When we introduce this framework as a 1-day workshop for leaders, we end the day with a "Commitment Wall" where all the participating leaders commit to take and action with their team in each of the three areas. The commitment anchors the learnings from the training and allow the leaders to bring it home and into their lives and work.

---

27       January 2025 numbers.

So, what is the Role of Compassion in Belonging?

Compassion is the foundation for belonging and amplifies belonging by fostering deeper connections and emotional safety. Compassionate leadership involves:

- Empathy: Taking the time to understand employees' challenges, needs and dreams.
- Action: Providing meaningful support and resources to address those needs.
- Accountability: Creating systems that balances well-being and equity with all the other ways of measuring business success.

For example, at Boston Scientific, leaders demonstrated compassion by actively listening to employee concerns during a period of organizational change. They implemented programs to enhance psychological safety and ensure employees felt valued and included. These efforts resulted in higher engagement scores and a stronger sense of belonging across teams.

Boston Scientific exemplifies the power of belonging. During a strategic initiative to work with Organizational Happiness, enhance workplace culture and performance, the organization focused on fostering inclusion and leveraging the "Seen, Contribute, Proud" model.

Key priorities included:

1. Leadership Training: Equipping managers with tools to recognize and celebrate individual strengths and fostering belonging.
2. Feedback Loops: Establishing channels for employees to share ideas and concerns, ensuring their voices were heard.
3. Purpose Alignment: Highlighting the organization's mission and values in daily operations, reinforcing a shared sense of pride.

These efforts led to measurable improvements in employee engagement and other HR KPIs. Boston Scientific's success demonstrates that belonging is not just an abstract concept but a tangible driver of business outcomes.

A university that I have worked with for over a decade, in one of the happiest countries in the world, Costa Rica, has a dedicated program to help leaders grow their muscle on fostering organizational happiness, compassion and belonging in their organizations: the "Organizational Happiness Certification Course" offered by the UPEACE Centre for Executive Education.[28]

This globally recognized certification includes dedicated modules on the "Power of Belonging" and "Compassion in Action". Participants are guided through reflections and practical strategies to embed these principles within

---

28 UPEACE, established and mandated by the United Nations in 1980, focuses on promoting understanding, tolerance, and peaceful coexistence.

their organizations. As part of both the "Global Leadership Diploma" and the "Diploma in Social Innovation", this course emphasizes:

1. The Science of Happiness: Rooted in positive psychology, this module explores the evidence-based foundations of happiness and belonging.
2. Practical Applications: Participants develop a personalized game plan to implement strategies for organizational happiness, belonging and compassion in their workplaces.
3. Global Impact: Graduates become part of an international network and tribe of changemakers dedicated to driving organizational happiness.

One of the course's unique features is its focus on moving from strategy to action. It equips leaders with the tools to measure, monitor, and adapt their initiatives to create a sustainable culture of Organizational Happiness. As a facilitator of this program, I have witnessed its transformative impact on leaders and organizations worldwide.

Creating a culture of belonging requires intentionality and action. Here are five strategies or actions leaders can be inspired by — and implement:

1. Cultivate Psychological Safety: Encourage open dialogue and make it safe for employees to express themselves without fear of judgment.

2.  Celebrate "Individuality": Recognize and leverage the unique strengths and perspectives each team member brings.

3.  Foster Connection: Facilitate opportunities for employees to build authentic relationships across teams and levels.

4.  Align Values and Purpose: Ensure organizational values are lived and celebrated, creating a shared sense of meaning

5.  Measure and Adapt: Regularly assess belonging through surveys and feedback, using insights to refine initiatives.

Compassion is the foundation of meaningful human connection. It is more than just an emotion—it is an action-oriented mindset that drives understanding, care, and support for others. In leadership, compassion transforms into compassionate leadership, where leaders actively prioritize the well-being of those they lead, creating environments where people feel valued, seen, and supported.

One of the most profound outcomes of compassionate leadership is belonging. When leaders lead with compassion, they foster a culture where individuals feel safe to contribute, express themselves, and engage fully in their work. Belonging is not just about inclusion—it's about creating a space where people know they matter, both as individuals and as part of a greater purpose.

---

Moreover, organizations that champion belonging often experience a direct correlation with innovation. Psychological safety - a vital component of belonging - allows employees to voice unconventional ideas without fear of rejection. This openness fuels creativity and empowers teams to tackle challenges with bold, collaborative solutions. When belonging becomes a cultural norm, organizations unlock their full potential, transforming challenges into opportunities.

Belonging extends beyond the workplace, shaping how individuals engage with their communities and families. Leaders who prioritize belonging inspire others to do the same, creating a ripple effect that contributes to a more compassionate and connected society.

---

My intention and hope are that this chapter inspires you to take action, fostering a culture of belonging that uplifts your organization and contributes to a better world.

Together, we can build workplaces where everyone feels seen, valued, and proud.

---

Belonging and psychological safety are closely tied to the concept of servant leadership, a philosophy that places the needs of others at the forefront of decision-making and action. Servant leaders approach their roles with humility, empathy, and a commitment to creating environments where individuals feel empowered, supported, and connected.

In the next chapter, we will explore how servant leadership transforms the principles of compassion and belonging into actionable strategies that cultivate extraordinary teams and sustainable success. This shift - from leading with authority to leading with service - is the essence of Compassion in Action, and it builds the foundation for the kind of leadership the world urgently needs today.

## The Leader as Servant

Servant leadership, a philosophy that puts the needs of others first, has gained prominence as an essential approach for creating high-performing, purpose-driven organizations. It takes for granted that people inherently want to make a difference and to perform — and the leadership job about releasing that potential.

At its core lies the belief that leadership is not about commanding authority, but about service and care.

As Robert K. Greenleaf once said, *"The servant-leader is servant first. It begins with the natural feeling that one wants to serve, to serve first."*

This philosophy is further reflected in the wisdom of Mahatma Gandhi: *"The best way to find yourself is to lose yourself in the service of others."*

Servant leadership asks leaders to look beyond themselves and prioritize the well-being and growth of their people. Simon Sinek echoes this sentiment: *"Leadership is not about being in charge. It is about taking care of those in your charge."*

For me, servant leadership is the foundational mindset that underpins leaders who practice Compassion in Action. I will use this chapter to explore the principles of servant leadership, its academic underpinnings, and actionable strategies for integrating this philosophy into modern organizational frameworks.

---

Servant leadership is a transformational leadership philosophy that puts the well-being and growth of others first. This philosophy is about fostering environments where people can thrive, rooted in care and empathy. It is the foundational mindset that underpins Compassion in Action.

# COMPASSION IN ACTION

"An interest in understanding other peoples difficulties and a burning desire to do something about it!"

*"Compassion in Action is about prioritizing the well-being of the people you lead and creating environments where individuals and organizations can thrive."*

This definition is critical in shaping leadership that is truly people-centered and purpose-driven.

## History and Academics:

The roots of servant leadership trace back to Robert K. Greenleaf's 1970 essay, *The Servant as Leader*. Inspired by Hermann Hesse's novel, *Journey to the East*, Greenleaf envisioned leadership as a relational practice that focuses on serving others to foster well-being and individual growth. His "servant-first" model continues to be foundational in understanding how leaders can inspire teams to thrive.

Larry Spears, a contemporary thought leader on servant leadership, expanded on Greenleaf's work by identifying ten characteristics, including listening, empathy, healing, awareness, persuasion, conceptualization, foresight, stewardship, commitment to growth, and building community.

The Dalai Lama reinforces this perspective by emphasizing the importance of altruism and oneness. He notes:

*"Reinstating a commitment to the oneness of humanity and altruism toward our brothers and sisters is fundamental for societies and organizations and their individuals to thrive in the long run."*

His words highlight the essential role of compassion in servant leadership.

Greenleaf's philosophy connects with the concept of purpose. Purpose aligns leaders with long-term goals that benefit not only their organizations but also their communities. Servant leaders help their teams discover and connect to purpose, fostering motivation and meaning in their work.

---

Servant leadership is not just a moral philosophy - it drives measurable outcomes in well-being, engagement, and organizational success.

Improved Well-Being: Organizations that embrace servant leadership report 78% higher morale and lower stress levels among employees. A Deloitte study found that servant-led workplaces create cultures of care and resilience, reducing burnout by 30%.

Thriving Workplaces: Servant leaders inspire environments where individuals bring their best selves to work. This fosters creativity, resilience, and long-term commitment.

Greater Innovation: Psychological safety, a hallmark of servant leadership, encourages teams to take risks and propose new ideas without fear of failure. Studies show that servant-led teams are 25% more innovative than those under traditional leadership styles.

**Key Performance Indicators (KPIs)**

Organizations practicing servant leadership can measure their impact through:

- Employee Retention Rates: A significant reduction in turnover indicates higher satisfaction and trust.
- Engagement Metrics: Servant-led teams consistently score higher on engagement surveys, reflecting increased motivation and collaboration.
- Customer Satisfaction: Happy employees translate to loyal customers, with companies like Southwest Airlines and Ritz-Carlton providing clear examples.

What Does Servant Leadership Look Like? Servant leadership is expressed through intentional behaviors that prioritize the well-being of employees. These behaviors transform organizations into thriving ecosystems where individuals and teams flourish.

Servant leadership requires consistent behaviors and systemic support. Here's what I think can make it successful in practice:

Be Mindful: The Dalai Lama stresses, *"Cultivate peace of mind. When the mind is compassionate, it is calm, enabling leaders to use their sense of reason with determination."* Mindfulness enhances clarity and decision-making.

Ask Questions Instead of Giving Commands: Foster autonomy by asking, "What do you need to succeed with

XX?" What do you need from me to be a success here. This approach shifts focus from control to empowerment.

Act as a role model: Ensure your behavior aligns with organizational values. This consistency builds trust and motivates employees to emulate the same standards.

Prioritize well-being, empowering others, and create environments where people and organizations thrive —as a motor for sustainable success.

By embedding servant leadership principles into daily practices, organizations can foster sustainable growth, trust, and resilience.

Servant leadership lays the groundwork for a leadership style rooted in service, humility, and empowerment. But beyond serving, leaders must also have the courage to step fully into their presence, strength, and responsibility.

This is where the Gentle Giant comes in - a leader who embodies both power and compassion, leading with authenticity, courage, and care. We will return to the Gentle Giant after examining four influential voices who have shaped the foundation of Compassion in Action.

# CHAPTER 5

# 4 Influential Voices

Great leadership is not developed in isolation. It is shaped by ideas, experiences, and the wisdom of esteemed thought leaders who have paved the way. Their groundbreaking work has been a personal inspiration to me in my journey as a change-maker, helping leaders and organizations integrate *Compassion in Action* into their leadership and cultures.

In this chapter, I introduce four influential thinkers whose insights, research, and proven frameworks deeply align with the principles of compassionate leadership. Each of them demonstrates that true leadership is built on trust, emotional intelligence, authenticity, and the ability to create environments where people thrive.

Their work has not only reinforced my belief that leadership is about service, purpose, and unlocking human potential—it has also shaped my approach to developing leaders and fostering **Organizational Happiness**. These thought leaders offer invaluable perspectives on what it means to lead with **compassion, courage, and impact**, showing that leadership is not just about strategy, but about creating meaningful, lasting change.

The four thought leaders featured in this chapter are:

1. **Brené Brown** – Expert on vulnerability, courage, and the power of authentic leadership.
2. **Kim Scott** – Developer of Radical Candor, a framework that combines caring personally with challenging directly.
3. **Pippa Grange** – Author of *Fear Less*, focusing on overcoming fear-based leadership and creating cultures of psychological safety and emotional resilience.
4. **Luis Gallardo** – Creator of Happytalism, a movement that redefines success by prioritizing happiness and well-being in leadership and business.

The strong connection between their work and Compassion in Action is clear:

- Vulnerability and courage (Brown) are essential for trust and deep connections in leadership.
- Radical honesty with care (Scott) is key to building healthy, high-performing teams.
- Overcoming fear in leadership (Grange) enables leaders to create environments of trust and psychological safety.
- Redefining leadership success (Gallardo) aligns perfectly with Compassion in Action's focus on well-being and sustainable performance.

I invite and encourage you to dive into their work, explore their insights, and apply their principles to your own leadership practice.

Let their ideas inspire you, challenge your thinking, and help you cultivate Compassion in Action in your leadership and organization.

## Dare to Lead

Great leadership is not about command and control - it is about courage, vulnerability, and genuine human connection.

In Dare to Lead, Brené Brown presents a transformative leadership framework that challenges leaders to embrace discomfort, uncertainty, and responsibility in creating workplaces built on trust and psychological safety.

Brené Brown's Daring Leadership Manifesto emphasizes that great leaders do not avoid difficult conversations or hide behind authority; they lead with authenticity and openness. They create environments where people feel safe to innovate, take risks, and contribute meaningfully. As she states, "Daring leaders are never silent about hard things."

This philosophy aligns closely with Compassion in Action, which calls on leaders to go beyond simply recognizing the struggles of those they serve to take intentional action that uplifts, supports, and empowers them.

Daring Leadership rejects outdated leadership models based on fear, hierarchy, and self-protection. Instead, Brené Brown challenge leaders to:

- Show up fully and be seen – Leadership is not about titles or maintaining distance. Great leaders engage, listen, and lead with authenticity.
- Embrace vulnerability and courage – Leadership is not about having all the answers but about creating space for questions, learning, and growth.
- Create psychological safety – Trust is built in small moments. Leaders must cultivate environments where people feel valued and safe to take risks.
- Turn empathy into action. Understanding people's challenges is only the first step; leaders must take meaningful action to support their teams.

A leader who dares to lead with compassion is one who empowers, elevates, and transforms those around them.

In *Dare to Lead*, Brown teaches that true courage is not about power - it is about leading with heart, setting boundaries, and standing in discomfort when necessary.

As leaders, we must:

- Dare to engage in difficult conversations.
- Dare to lead with heart, not ego.
- Dare to create workplaces where people feel safe, seen, and supported.

Brene Brown reminds us:

*"Clear is kind. Unclear is unkind."*

Brené Brown also emphasises that compassionate leadership calls for clarity - clear expectations, honest feedback, and decisive action to ensure people are supported, not just managed.

*"True leadership is not about avoiding discomfort - it is about leaning into it with courage and care."*

In short, leaders must cultivate workplaces where people feel valued, inspired, and empowered to do their best work by:

- Having the courage to be vulnerable.
- Create spaces where people thrive.
- Lead with compassion, not fear.

By daring to lead with compassion, we facilitate thriving organizations and sustainable success - and a world where leadership is a force for good.

Another inspiration for me on daring and courage is Whatson Institute in Boulder whose philosophy starts with "Protect your courage".[29] Which have fostered many of their students to engage in new groundbreaking adventures where some might change the world just a little bit.

---

29 Watson Institute. (n.d.). Our Philosophy: Protect Your Courage. Retrieved from [Watson Institute Website]

## Radical Candor

Radical Candor and Compassion in Action: A Balanced Leadership Approach.

Kim Scott, the creator of *Radical Candor*, defines it as "Caring Personally while Challenging Directly," striking a balance between honest feedback and genuine concern for people's well-being.[30]

She advocates for leadership that is transparent, compassionate, and action driven.

*"Saying what you think while also giving a damn about the person you're saying it to."*

The model is built on two key components:

- Caring Personally — Leaders must show genuine concern for their employees beyond their work performance.
- Challenging Directly — Leaders must provide clear, honest feedback that helps individuals grow and improve.

Radical Candor ensures that feedback is neither passive nor aggressive. It prevents leaders from falling into Ruinous Empathy (being too nice and avoiding criticism) or Obnoxious

---

30 1. Scott, K. (2017). Radical Candor: Be a Kick-Ass Boss Without Losing Your Humanity. St. Martin's Press. 2. Scott, K. (2021). "How to Give Feedback the Radical Candor Way." Retrieved from radicalcandor.com

Aggression (being too blunt without care). Instead, it fosters a culture of open, trust-based communication where feedback is expected, valued, and constructive.

While Radical Candor becomes an inspiration on honest communication, I believe we should take it one step further and move beyond communication and words to meaningful action.

Compassionate leadership is not passive sympathy; it is proactive and ensures well-being, belonging, and personal growth. It is about:

- Understanding employees' challenges and addressing them with meaningful solutions.
- Creating psychological safety so people feel free to express themselves and take risks without fear.
- Taking responsibility as a leader to remove obstacles that hinder individual and collective success.

Although they come from different perspectives, Radical Candor and Compassion in Action complement each other perfectly:

Radical Candor ensures honesty → Compassion in Action ensures care and action.

Radical Candor fosters open communication → Compassion in Action ensures those conversations lead to meaningful change.

Radical Candor helps people grow → Compassion in Action supports them in the process.

Together, these approaches create a balanced leadership style one that is both strong and compassionate, truthful and supportive. A leader who integrates both can deliver difficult feedback without harming relationships, challenge employees while maintaining trust, and cultivate a workplace where accountability and well-being go hand in hand.

The Courage to Lead with Compassion and Honesty.

Leadership requires both courage and care.

By integrating Radical Candor and Compassion in Action, leaders unlock the full human potential of their teams and organizations.

## Fear Less

Dr. Pippa Grange's *Fear Less: How to Win at Life Without Losing Yourself* presents a compelling perspective on overcoming fear as a core leadership challenge.

Her work has opened my eyes to yet another dimension of compassionate leadership—one that explores the profound impact of leading without fear.

Pippa Grange argues that fear is one of the most limiting forces in leadership and performance - not because it exists, but because of how we respond to it. Rather than using fear as a motivator through competition, perfectionism, or rigid control, she encourages leaders to replace fear with connection, purpose, and courage.

A central message in *Fear Less* is that leaders must move away from fear-based control and toward values-driven leadership. Pippa states that many organizations still operate under outdated models that rely on pressure, competition, and dominance, believing these elements enhance performance.

Pippa Grange challenges this notion, arguing that it leads to burnout, disengagement, and insecurity.

Pippa Grange identifies two primary types of fear that hold people back:

1. In-the-Moment Fear – The instinctual fear that triggers a survival response.
2. Not-Good-Enough Fear – A deeper, more pervasive fear that drives perfectionism, self-doubt, and a scarcity mindset.

Fear-based cultures manifest through excessive competition, unrealistic expectations, and constant pressure to prove oneself.

When organizations shift from fear to compassion, engagement and well-being increase, while stress and burnout decrease.

Pippa Grange highlights that to eliminate fear-based leadership, leaders must replace fear with purpose, connection, and emotional resilience. She suggests several ways to achieve this:

- Shift from individual success to collective success – Moving from external validation and competition to fulfillment through shared purpose and collaboration.
- Foster human connection – Encouraging vulnerability, honesty, and trust in leadership relationships.
- Build a strong inner foundation – Developing self-compassion to enhance resilience and emotional intelligence.

## The Fear Less Manifesto and the Future of Leadership

She concludes *Fear Less* with the *Fear Less Manifesto*, calling on leaders to reject fear-based leadership and embrace courage, purpose, and connection.

Pippa Grange's *Fear Less* and *Compassion in Action* share a common mission: to redefine leadership beyond fear and control and toward courage, empathy, and genuine human connection.

When leaders replace fear with compassion, trust, and empowerment, they unlock not only higher performance but also deeper fulfillment and meaning.

## Happytalism

Through my work with Compassion in Action and compassionate leadership, I have come to understand that truly making a difference requires a fundamental shift - from profit-driven models to people-centered approaches that place happiness, well-being, and purpose at the core of leadership and organizational success.

As organizations navigate increasing complexity, uncertainty, and rapid change, there is a growing realization that traditional capitalist models focused primarily on financial gain often fall short in fostering sustainable success. Instead, a more holistic and human-centered approach is needed - one that aligns business success with societal well-being.

A great model for how this shift can be perceived is made by Luis Gallardo in his book on Happytalism. He challenges traditional capitalism by redefining progress, focusing on happiness rather than solely financial metrics. It promotes well-being as a primary goal, conscious leadership, and purpose-driven freedom. Luis Gallardo, is the founder of the World Happiness Foundation and a key advocate of Happytalism, describes it as a socio-economic development system that places happiness and well-being at the center of human progress.[31]

Happytalism is not just a theoretical concept; it provides a framework for rethinking leadership, organizational

---

31 Gallardo, L. (2021). Happytalism: The Future of Capitalism. World Happiness Foundation.

structures, and the way success is measured. Instead of relying purely on profit margins or shareholder returns, it encourages organizations to consider how they contribute to human flourishing. Businesses, governments, and institutions that adopt this approach shift their focus from short-term financial performance to long-term sustainability, employee well-being, and broader societal impact.

I see Happytalism as providing the macro-level vision of a world where happiness and well-being are central to progress. Complementing this, Compassion in Action serves as a practical leadership framework, equipping leaders with the tools and behaviors needed to bring this vision to life within organizations. My goal is to help leaders integrate well-being and purpose into their daily leadership practices—because small, consistent actions taken by many leaders across many organizations can collectively create a meaningful, positive impact on the world. And isn't that a vision worth striving for?

Compassion in Action builds on the core principles of Happytalism in several ways:

1. Turning Vision into Daily Leadership Practices – Happytalism provides a broad vision of leadership centered on happiness and well-being, but organizations need clear, actionable steps to bring this vision into their culture. Compassion in Action provides a structured leadership approach that embeds well-being into daily decision-making, interactions, and management practices.

2. Prioritizing Well-Being as a Strategic Imperative – Both frameworks emphasize that well-being should not be an afterthought or a separate initiative but a fundamental driver of organizational success. Compassion in Action provides a way for leaders to make well-being a strategic priority, ensuring that it influences every aspect of the business, from talent development to decision-making processes.

3. Building Psychological Safety and Trust – One of the key ideas in Happytalism is the role of conscious leadership in fostering environments where people feel valued and fulfilled. Compassion in Action operationalizes this by helping leaders create cultures of psychological safety, where employees feel secure in expressing ideas, taking risks, and collaborating openly.

4. Balancing Purpose with Performance – Happytalism emphasizes the need for organizations to be purpose-driven. Compassion in Action helps leaders align business objectives with a greater sense of purpose, ensuring that teams feel motivated not just by financial goals but by a deeper mission that contributes to positive societal impact.

5. Driving Sustainable Success through People-Centered Leadership – Compassion in Action aligns with Happytalism's belief that human well-being drives long-term business success. By leading with compassion, fostering inclusive workplaces, and

supporting employees holistically, organizations unlock engagement, creativity, and resilience—ultimately outperforming those that rely solely on transactional leadership methods.

The evolution from traditional capitalism to Happytalism, reinforced by Compassion in Action, marks a significant shift in leadership thinking. It is no longer enough to focus on financial growth alone; organizations must cultivate environments where people thrive. Happytalism lays the groundwork for this shift by redefining success, while Compassion in Action ensures that leaders have the necessary mindset, behaviors, and frameworks to implement it effectively.

By integrating the principles of Happytalism with the leadership approach of Compassion in Action, organizations create thriving ecosystems where well-being, engagement, and sustainable success go hand in hand. This is the future of leadership—one that values human potential as the most important asset for building long-term prosperity.

# CHAPTER 6

# The Gentle Giants

*A Role Model and Lighthouse
for Compassion in Action*

Great leadership is not about dominance or control; it is about strength, service, and compassion. As I've emphasized throughout this book, I deeply believe in compassionate leadership. Over the course of my work, I've had the privilege of meeting leaders who don't just practice compassionate leadership—they embody it. They serve as powerful role models, demonstrating what it truly means to lead with empathy, strength, and purpose. I want to share their qualities with you as both inspiration and a call to action—an invitation to step into their footsteps, embrace Compassion in Action, and become a Gentle Giant in your own leadership journey.

The Gentle Giant represents a leader who stands tall, leads with confidence, and uses their power with purpose - not for personal gain but for the well-being of others.

A Gentle Giant doesn't shrink or hide their influence. Instead, they step fully into their leadership, balancing courage with humility, wisdom with empathy, and power with purpose.

They recognize that Compassion in Action is not weakness - it is the highest form of strength.

At the beginning of this book, I shared my belief that we are at the edge of a leadership revolution—a shift that demands more humanity and compassion in leadership.

As I said in the very beginning of this book, "The next big revolution isn't driven by technology—it's driven by more humanity and compassion in leadership. Our real problems aren't technological; they are moral and ethical."

This revolution requires all the Gentle Giants we can muster.

A Gentle Giant leads with strengths, service and compassion, embracing their influence not to control, but to empower.

They create trust, psychological safety, and a culture where people thrive.

Strength with Humility – Power is used to uplift, not dominate.

Compassion with Action – Leadership is about understanding and doing something about it.

"We take care of the well-being of the people we serve and lead.

It's an obligation.

And we understand that it's a huge opportunity for sustainable success for the organization we are responsible for.

We are GENTLE GIANTS."

Courage with Purpose – Leading with heart, integrity, and a focus on sustainable success.

Confidence Without Ego – They lead not for personal validation, but for the greater good.

Gentle Giants do not seek control, validation, or power for its own sake. They are secure in their leadership and understand that the true measure of success is how well they support and uplift others. They know that leadership is not about them - it's about the people they serve.

This is your invitation to step into a new kind of leadership - one that inspires, serves, and creates lasting impact.

I invite you to embrace:

Authenticity – Own your strengths and lead with confidence, not arrogance.

Compassion – Truly care for the people you lead and take intentional action to support them.

Trust – Foster psychological safety and allow people to contribute their best.

Service – Lead not for status, but to serve something greater than yourself.

Courage – Dare to lead with heart. Challenge old paradigms and build something better.

Don't let anyone take your kindness for weakness.

To empower leaders to embrace Compassion in Action and take meaningful steps forward, I have created *The Gentle Giant Manifesto* - a set of core principles, commitments, and a call to action.

This manifesto is more than just a guide; it is an invitation to step into leadership with wisdom, kindness, and purpose. It is a call to join a movement of leaders who choose to lead with strength, compassion, and integrity -a community and a tribe dedicated to shaping a better future by fostering trust, inspiring others, and creating lasting impact.

This is not just a philosophy - it is a call to action. Whether in business, government, or society, leaders who embrace Compassion in Action will define the next era of leadership.

# The Gentle Giant Manifesto

*Guiding Principles for Leaders Committed
to Compassion in Action.*

Real leadership is not about dominance or control - it is about creating a future where humanity, well-being, and sustainable success for our organizations are at the heart of every decision.

As Gentle Giants, we lead with strength and purpose while embracing Compassion in Action as our guiding force.

We take care of the well-being of the people we serve and lead - not as an afterthought, but as a strategic priority. Because when people thrive, organizations flourish, and societies prosper.

*The 3 Core Principles of a Gentle Giant*

## 1. Compassion in Action is Our Leadership Paradigm

Compassion is not a passive emotion - it is a leadership discipline. It is an interest in understanding the difficulties of others and a burning desire to do something about it.

We don't just care - we act.

## 2. The Happiness Sweet Spot as Our Foundation

We recognize that The Happiness Sweet Spot is the foundation for sustainable leadership and thriving organizations. It serves as the enabling platform that empowers individuals and teams to perform at their when we align and integrate:

- PURPOSE – The deeper reason we exist and lead beyond profit.
- STRENGTHS – Unlocking and developing the unique potential of our people.
- COMPASSION – Creating a culture where trust, belonging, and engagement thrive.

## 3. We Lead with Courage, Not Ego

True leadership is about serving, not controlling. It is about unlocking and releasing the potential already within the organization, not forcing transformation. We focus on:

Asking the right questions rather than pretending to have all the answers.

Building trust and psychological safety to empower innovation and growth.

Creating environments where people feel Seen, Contribute, and are Proud - the foundation of belonging.

Make others shine.

## *The Gentle Giant <u>Commitment</u>*

We take care of the well-being of the people we serve and lead. It's our responsibility and our greatest opportunity for sustainable success.

We put people at the center of progress. Technology and strategy matter, but real success is built on humanity and ethical leadership.

We make Compassion in Action a clear strategic priority. Not as a program, but as the very foundation of how we lead and operate.

We embrace simplicity and clarity. Complexity is the enemy of execution. We focus on what truly matters - enabling people, driving engagement, and ensuring sustainable impact.

We dare to lead with both strength and heart. Because the future belongs to those who step up, challenge the status quo, and lead with compassion and courage.

**Join the tribe - Be a Gentle Giant**

# CHAPTER 7

# Self-Compassion

Through my work in engaging, coaching, leadership development, and training, I have had countless conversations with leaders about tapping into the power of Compassion in Action as a new leadership paradigm. More often than not, these discussions lead to a deeper, sometimes vulnerable reflection on self-compassion.

Many leaders quietly ask, "Who can I talk to? What about me? I need compassion too." The truth is, leading with compassion starts with extending that same compassion to ourselves. Leadership comes with immense responsibility, and yet, leaders often overlook their own need for understanding, care, and support.

Very often, we as leaders hold ourselves to higher standards than the people we lead and serve. We demand more from ourselves, expecting perfection, resilience, and unwavering strength. Our inner voice can be quite harsh—and not very compassionate. Instead of the kindness and encouragement we readily offer others, we are often our own worst critics.

One place to begin is by reflecting on your own self-compassion practices—how you treat yourself in moments of challenge, failure, or uncertainty. Another is to find someone to hold your hand along the way—whether that's a mentor, a coach, or a trusted peer.

Self-compassion is not about indulgence; it's about sustaining your ability to lead with clarity, resilience, and strength. In this chapter, we will explore why self-compassion is essential for leadership, how it directly influences our ability to lead others, and practical ways to integrate it into daily leadership practice.

This topic could easily fill an entire book on its own, and I recognize that this chapter alone may not fully do justice to the immense importance of self-compassion for leaders who commit to igniting Compassion in Action and stepping into the role of a Gentle Giant.

Self-compassion is the foundation of true well-being and a critical building block for Compassion in Action.

I have always believed that you cannot truly practice compassion for others without first practicing self-compassion. However, research suggests otherwise - while it is possible to extend compassion to others without self-compassion, it often comes at a cost.

I have seen this firsthand, particularly in NGO and social entrepreneurship environments. Leaders in these spaces dedicate themselves fully to serving others, yet many do so while neglecting their own well-being. While this can work in the short term, it often leads to burnout, exhaustion, and emotional depletion.

---

This chapter will explore the academic foundations of self-compassion, its importance for leaders, practical strategies to develop it, and how it integrates into Compassion In Action.

---

Self-compassion has been increasingly recognized in academic and professional contexts as a key element of resilience and adaptability. Serena Chen's research highlights that self-compassion not only helps individuals recover from setbacks but also fosters a growth mindset—the belief that abilities and skills can be developed with effort. This mindset is essential for leaders who aim to innovate and improve continuously. Additionally, self-compassion enhances authenticity, allowing individuals to align their actions with their core values, which is vital for effective leadership.

Stephanie Harrison's work expands on these ideas by providing a practical framework for developing self-compassion, emphasizing the importance of treating oneself with kindness and acknowledging the shared human experience of struggle. This approach helps leaders reduce self-critical tendencies and improve emotional well-being, ultimately fostering stronger, more adaptable teams.

Defined by Dr. Kristin Neff, a pioneer in the field, self-compassion involves treating oneself with the same kindness, care, and understanding that one would offer a close friend during difficult times.

Dr. Neff's research identifies three core components of self-compassion: "self-kindness", "common humanity", and "mindfulness". Self-kindness encourages leaders to avoid harsh self-criticism and instead approach themselves with warmth and support. Common humanity emphasizes the shared experience of struggle, helping leaders understand that imperfection is a natural part of life. Mindfulness involves maintaining balanced awareness of emotions, preventing over-identification with negativity.

Research consistently highlights the benefits of self-compassion. Leaders with higher levels of self-compassion demonstrate greater resilience, improved emotional intelligence, and reduced levels of stress and burnout.

---

Self-compassion is not self-indulgence; it is a strategy for sustainable performance. Leaders often prioritize the needs of others over their own, leading to burnout and diminished effectiveness. By practicing self-compassion, leaders build emotional resilience and create a positive ripple effect on their teams and organizations.

1.  Enhances Decision-Making: Leaders who practice self-compassion are less likely to be paralyzed by fear of failure, enabling them to take calculated risks and innovate.

2.  Strengthens Relationships: Self-compassionate leaders exhibit higher levels of empathy and emotional intelligence, fostering trust and psychological safety within teams.

3.  Promotes Sustainable Leadership: Self-compassion buffers against stress and prevents burnout, allowing leaders to sustain high performance over the long term.

4.  Encourages a Growth Mindset: Self-compassion triggers a growth mindset, motivating leaders to learn from mistakes and continuously improve.

5.  Authenticity and Adaptability: Leaders who practice self-compassion align their actions with their core values, enhancing authenticity and adaptability in their roles.

---

Stephanie Harrison's CARE framework provides actionable steps to build self-compassion:

1.  Catch Yourself Being Critical: Acknowledge and name your critical inner thoughts. For example, instead of allowing self-doubt to spiral, recognize it as a passing thought.

2.  Acknowledge Your Experiences: Validate your emotions and accept that setbacks are part of the

human experience. This practice helps leaders process challenges constructively.

3. Request Compassion: Ask yourself what a supportive friend would say in your situation. Repeat mantras like, "I am allowed to make mistakes," or "I am capable of growth."

4. Explore the Next Step: Use self-compassion as a springboard for problem-solving. For instance, after a mistake, reflect on practical ways to improve without self-recrimination.

By incorporating the CARE framework into daily routines, leaders can cultivate resilience and clarity in their decision-making processes.

---

### Here is an Invitation to Explore What Works for You

Cultivating self-compassion is a deeply personal journey, and what works for one person may not resonate with another. Here is an invitation to play with these practices, experiment with different approaches, and discover what feels most supportive and effective for you.

To help establish self-compassion as a habit, consider drawing inspiration from the framework outlined in James Clear's "Atomic Habits". Building effective habits requires:

1.  Make It Obvious: Identify clear cues for your self-compassion practice, such as setting a daily reminder to reflect or journal.
2.  Make It Attractive: Link the habit to something you enjoy or value, such as pairing mindfulness with a walk in nature.
3.  Make It Easy: Start small—commit to just five minutes of reflection or breathing exercises each day.
4.  Make It Satisfying: Reward yourself for practicing self-compassion, even if it's a simple acknowledgment of your effort.

By approaching self-compassion with intentionality and structure, you can integrate it seamlessly into your routine and experience lasting benefits for both your personal well-being and leadership effectiveness. The key is to make self-compassion a habit—integrate it into your daily life and observe what practices truly enhance your well-being and resilience.

## 11 Things You Can Do

Self-compassion is not just a mindset—it requires intentional practice. Leaders can integrate self-compassion into their daily routines using these 11 practical strategies to build resilience, emotional intelligence, and sustainable leadership habits.

**1. Engage in Regular Movement:** Physical activity plays a crucial role in mental and emotional well-being. Whether it's walking, stretching, yoga, or strength training, movement helps reduce stress, improve focus, and foster clarity. Exercise releases endorphins, counteracting stress and improving emotional balance.

*Practical Tip: Schedule small movement breaks throughout the day—stand up and stretch between meetings, take a short walk, or incorporate mindful movement like yoga into your routine.*

**2. Practice Deep Breathing:** Controlled breathing helps regulate the nervous system, reducing stress and increasing mental clarity. Techniques such as box breathing (inhale for four seconds, hold for four seconds, exhale for four seconds) or the 4-7-8 method (inhale for four seconds, hold for seven, exhale for eight) can have a significant impact.

*Practical Tip: Before a high-pressure meeting or difficult conversation, take five deep breaths to ground yourself and enhance focus.*

**3. Spend Time in Nature:** Spending time outdoors reduces stress and fosters mental clarity. Whether taking a walk in a park, hiking, or simply sitting by a body of water, nature helps put challenges into perspective and fosters a sense of calm.

*Practical Tip: Take 10–15 minutes outside during the workday or try a "walking meditation" to reconnect with your surroundings and reset your mind.*

**4. Incorporate Mindfulness Practices:** Mindfulness helps leaders cultivate present-moment awareness, reducing reactivity and increasing clarity in decision-making. Practicing mindfulness allows leaders to approach challenges with a balanced perspective.

*Practical Tip: Set aside five to ten minutes a day for mindfulness meditation, breathwork, or focused attention exercises to develop emotional balance.*

**5. Write a Self-Compassion Letter:** Many leaders hold themselves to high standards and struggle with self-criticism. Writing a self-compassion letter helps shift the inner dialogue from self-judgment to self-support.

*Practical Tip: Reflect on a recent challenge and write to yourself as if you were offering encouragement to a close friend, highlighting lessons learned and offering self-kindness.*

**6. Acknowledge and Name Your Emotions:** Ignoring or suppressing emotions leads to stress and exhaustion. Instead of pushing aside difficult feelings, acknowledge them without judgment.

*Practical Tip: Try the RAIN method: Recognize, Allow, Investigate, and Nurture—an approach that helps process emotions in a healthy way.*

**7. Practice Gratitude:** Shifting focus from problems to gratitude improves resilience and overall well-being. Keeping a gratitude practice trains the mind to recognize positive aspects of leadership and life.

*Practical Tip: At the start or end of each day, write down three things you are grateful for. Consider also expressing gratitude in leadership settings by acknowledging team members' contributions.*

**8. Set and Enforce Boundaries:** Leaders often overextend themselves, leading to exhaustion and burnout. Setting clear boundaries is an essential act of self-compassion.

*Practical Tip: Before committing to a new project or request, ask yourself whether it aligns with your priorities and energy levels. Practice saying no with confidence when necessary.*

**9. Celebrate Small Wins:** High-achieving leaders often focus on what's next without recognizing their achievements. Taking time to celebrate small successes builds motivation and self-worth.

*Practical Tip: Keep a success journal where you note daily or weekly accomplishments, no matter how small.*

**10. Use Self-Compassion Mantras**: Words shape thoughts, and thoughts shape behavior. Repeating positive affirmations helps reframe negative thinking patterns.

*Practical Tip: Try mantras such as:*
- *"I am enough."*
- *"I am doing my best, and that is enough."*
- *"I deserve the same kindness I offer others."*

**11. Build a Support Network:** Leadership can be isolating, but having a strong support system provides guidance, encouragement, and perspective.

*Practical Tip: Identify three to five trusted people (mentors, colleagues, or peers) whom you can turn to for honest conversations, reflection, and support.*

---

Leaders who integrate self-compassion into their leadership practice experience greater resilience, emotional intelligence, and clarity, which in turn helps create work environments that foster trust, psychological safety, and engagement.

Self-compassion is not about self-indulgence - it is an essential leadership skill. It helps leaders sustain high performance, navigate setbacks with grace, and lead with greater impact.

---

By starting with self-compassion, as outlined in this chapter, leaders develop the emotional resilience and authenticity needed to effectively lead others. This foundation ensures that each step in the framework is grounded in empathy, clarity, and purpose.

Self-compassion is integral to Compassion in Action. Leaders who practice self-compassion are better equipped to extend compassion to others, fostering a culture of trust and belonging.

This chapter invites leaders to embark on a journey of self-discovery and growth, recognizing that the ability to lead others begins with the ability to lead oneself with compassion. Together, let us redefine leadership as an act of service, driven by self-awareness, empathy, and a commitment to creating environments where everyone can thrive and do their best.

# Closing Remarks

This book gives you a recipe for sustainable success, based on science, research, cases, our models, and tools. Together with the Happiness Sweet Spot and Motivational Landscape, this book is also a platform for inspiration and co-creation.

Use it and share it. We want to share our ideas, tell you what really works, and inspire you to start the organizational happiness journey for your team and your organization.

And we encourage you to share your story and insight with us. That way we – together - can catalyze and facilitate a movement that makes a difference by developing happy, sustainable, successful organizations and helps people and nations to thrive.

Find our partners and me on our websites, and feel free to contact me and the team directly at:

Lars@GntlGiant.com
www.GntlGiant.com

# The 10 messages

To make it easy to share and communicate the key insights from this book, here are the 10 core messages:

1. "The next big revolution isn't driven by technology—it's driven by more humanity and compassion in leadership. Our real problems aren't technological; they are moral and ethical."

2. "Be a Servant Leader. Be in Service to the future. Be a Gentle Giant."

3. "We take care of the well-being of the people we serve and lead. It's an obligation. And we understand that it's a huge opportunity for sustainable success for the organization we are responsible for: We are Gentle Giants."

4. "Compassion in Action and Organizational Happiness aren't just another "well-being program". It has to be a clear strategic priority. It's about tapping into the power of The Happiness Sweet Spot and truly taking care of the well-being of the people we lead and serve. It's both an obligation and a huge opportunity and motor for sustainable success for the organizations we're responsible for."

5. "Your real, unique competitive advantage is in your Purpose, your Culture and how you Manage and Lead your people".

6.  "It's already there! Compassion In Action is a powerful key to unlock and release the potential in your organization. Great leadership is not about transformation. Great leadership is about unlocking and releasing potential. This is the real motor for transformation. And a motor for sustainable success."

7.  Compassion In Action is "An interest in understanding other peoples difficulties - and a burning desire to do something about it!"

8.  "The Power Of Belonging: Seen, Contribute & Proud."

9.  "Follow those who ask the right questions, not those who claim to have all the answers."

10. "Getting from Strategy -> Action! The Answer Is : Simple! Complexity is the enemy of execution."

# Acknowledgments

This book has been years in the making—an incredible journey filled with extraordinary people, inspiring conversations, and transformative moments. It's been shaped by the wisdom, passion, and generosity of so many along the way!

A big *thank-you!* to the organizations, leaders, and people with whom I have served and worked. Thank you for the inspiration and for your trust. This book is really about you - and for you.

This book was born in the heart of the Serengeti, nurtured by the wisdom and generosity of an extraordinary leader. A heartfelt thank you to *Mama Zara*, Zainab Ansell - a true Gentle Giant of East Africa. For over a decade, I have followed and been inspired by her unwavering dedication, strength, and compassion. Her leadership exemplifies what it means to uplift others, create meaningful impact, and lead with both heart and purpose.

A heartfelt thank you to Tobias for your invaluable support and keen eye for visuals.

A sincere thank you to my friend and collaborator, Mohit, for your unwavering inspiration, partnership, and invaluable contributions. Your insights, dedication, and ability to challenge and refine ideas have been instrumental in developing frameworks and bringing depth to this work. As a trusted sounding board, your perspective has enriched this journey, and I am grateful for the wisdom and collaboration we continue to share.

To Lotte, my Angel - thank you for supporting my dreams, believing in me, and always insisting on brilliance. Your unconditional love is magical for me. You are a true unicorn.

*My Desk in Serengeti*

# Bibliography


Achor, S. (2012). *The happiness dividend. Harvard Business Review*, January/February.

Barsade, S. G., & O'Neill, O. A. (2014). *Employees who feel love perform better. Harvard Business Review.*

Bersin, J. *A new market is born.*

Brown, B. (2010). *The gifts of imperfection: Let go of who you think you're supposed to be and embrace who you are.* Hazelden Publishing.

Brown, B. (2012). *Daring greatly: How the courage to be vulnerable transforms the way we live, love, parent, and lead.* Gotham.

Brown, B. (2018). *Dare to lead: Brave work. Tough conversations. Whole hearts.* Random House.

Brown, B. *Daring leadership manifesto.* Retrieved from https://brenebrown.com.

Center for Talent Innovation (CTI). *Power of belonging: Key findings.*

Chapman, A. *The power of belonging - Workplace well-being professional. Workplace Well-being.*

Chen, S. (2021). *Give yourself a break: The power of self-compassion. Harvard Business Review*. Retrieved from https://hbr.org.

Clear, J. (2018). *Atomic habits: An easy & proven way to build good habits & break bad ones*. Penguin Random House.

Duhigg, C. (2016). *What Google learned from its quest to build the perfect team. The New York Times*.

Edmondson, A. C. (2019). *The fearless organization: Creating psychological safety in the workplace for learning, innovation, and growth*. Wiley.

EY Global. *How can you illuminate the power of belonging? Ernst & Young*.

Forbes. (2021). *What it takes to create a culture of belonging*.

Gallardo, L. (2021). *Happytalism: The future of capitalism. World Happiness Foundation*.

Grange, P. (2020). *Fear less: How to win at life without losing yourself*. Vermilion.

Grange, P. (2020). *The fear less manifesto*. Vermilion.

Heidrick & Struggles. *The CEO report: Embracing the paradoxes of leadership and the power of doubt*.

Harrison, S. (2021). *What does self-compassion really mean? Harvard Business Review*.

Juul, L. K. *The value of belonging at work (The power of belonging)*.

Kegan, R., & Lahey, L. L. (2016). *An everyone culture: Becoming a deliberately developmental organization. Harvard Business Review Press.*

National Institute of Mental Health. *Prevalence of any mental illness*.

Neff, K. (2003). *Self-compassion: Stop beating yourself up and leave insecurity behind.* HarperCollins.

Patagonia. *Company information & mission statement.* Retrieved from https://www.patagonia.com/company-info.html.

PepsiCo. (2013). *Mission statement.* Retrieved from http://www.pepsico.com.

Schein, E. H. (2017). *Humble leadership: The power of relationships, openness, and trust.* Berrett-Koehler Publishers.

Scott, K. (2017). *Radical candor: Be a kick-ass boss without losing your humanity.* St. Martin's Press.

Scott, K. (2021). *How to give feedback the radical candor way.* Retrieved from https://www.radicalcandor.com.

Seligman, M. (2011). *Flourish: A visionary new understanding of happiness and well-being.* Free Press.

Sull, D. N., & Eisenhardt, K. M. (2015). *How to thrive in a complex world.*

University for Peace (UPEACE). *Global organizational happiness certification programme.* Retrieved from https://centre.upeace.org.

Watson Institute. *Our philosophy: Protect your courage.* Retrieved from https://watson.is

World Happiness Report. (2024). *The role of happiness in economic development.*